The Other
PEARL HARBOR

JOHN MARTIN MEEK

The Other
PEARL HARBOR

The Army Air Corps &
Its Heroes on Dec. 7, 1941

TATE PUBLISHING & *Enterprises*

Published by Tate Publishing & Enterprises, LLC
127 E. Trade Center Terrace | Mustang, Oklahoma 73064 USA
1.888.361.9473 | www.tatepublishing.com

Tate Publishing is committed to excellence in the publishing industry. The company reflects the philosophy established by the founders, based on Psalm 68:11,
"The Lord gave the word and great was the company of those who published it."

Book design copyright © 2011 by Tate Publishing, LLC. All rights reserved.

On cover, from left, then 2nd Lt. Kenneth M. Taylor and 2nd Lt. George S Welch, U.S. Army Air Corps, with the Distinguished Service Cross medal both were awarded for their heroism during the Pearl Harbor attack . U.S. Army Air Corps photograph.

Cover design by Amber Gulilat
Interior design by Nathan Harmony

Published in the United States of America

ISBN: 978-1-61346-765-7
History / Military / World War II
11.09.12

Dedication

On Jan. 8, 1985, the Washington Post ran a headline in its "Obituaries" that read, "T.H. Dyer, Unsung Hero of World War II, Dies." For more than 23 years I have kept that yellowed old clipping on my desk until I could find an appropriate way to honor him.

A retired Navy captain, according to the Post obituary, Dyer was one of the cryptologists in the Navy's highly secret unit at Pearl Harbor who broke the Japanese code. He and his colleagues gave the Navy high command in the Pacific information leading to success in the important battles of the Coral Sea and at Midway, valuable Japanese merchant shipping information and, in what must have been a moment of sweet revenge, deciphered Adm. Isoruku Yamamoto's itinerary thus allowing U.S. aircraft to shoot down his plane over the Solomon Islands in the spring of 1943. And through their work Capt. Dyer and his associates doubtless saved thousands of lives including that of my brother, Dow Meek, who survived the sinking of the U.S.S. Yorktown in the Battle of Midway.

It is to Capt. Thomas H. Dyer, the unsung hero, that this book is dedicated. Thank you, Captain. Well done.

Acknowledgements

The idea for this work was suggested by Daniel Martinez, Pearl Harbor historian, when we had dinner in Honolulu one evening in May, 2007. I had never thought of doing a book on Ken Taylor and George Welch and had I done so, certainly would have started it while Gen. Taylor was alive and available to check various details other than what I already knew about Dec. 7, 1941.

In Ken's absence since his death Nov. 25, 2006, I have relied on Maj. Gen. Gordon Austin USAF Ret., commander of the 47th Pursuit Squadron at the time of the Pearl Harbor attack. Gen. Austin has not only been available for interviews, calls and personal visits but also loaned me his files of that time.

Others who were willing to assist over the years include Judy Bowman, Curator of the U.S. Army Museum of Hawaii, various staff members of the National Archives in College Park, MD, the Air Force Historical Agency at Maxwell AFB in Alabama and the microfilm staff at the Hawaii State Library in Honolulu.

Gen. Taylor's wife, Flora Love, provided the compelling evidence of Ken and George's first hero status when she loaned me a scrapbook Ken's mother had kept of his career, a literal gold mine of her son's early Air Corps service. It is about five inches thick with large varnished plywood covers and long brass grommets holding it together. On the front cover a skilled artist painted the logo of Brooks Field where Ken received his wings and commission as a second lieutenant.

Late in the writing of the book there was a serendipitous phone call to John Monahan, a long-time friend in Chicago, who revealed he had a collection of Life and Look magazines dating back to the Pearl Harbor attack time frame. He loaned them to me, yet another gold mine of information I found most useful–notably for a full-page photo of the newly minted hero, 2nd Lt. George Welch, surrounded by top starlets in Hollywood including Betty Grable, Claudette Colbert, Carole Landis and Ruth Hussey.

Another valued friend in Chicago, Lollie McKeon, not only read the manuscript for errors but made helpful suggestions as well.

A former fellow student at the University of Oklahoma, Richard Wentworth, who served many years as the director of the prestigious University of Illinois Press, provided much advice and counsel.

Another friend of many years in Washington, DC, Rick Barry, who was a Navy pilot during the Vietnam War era, read the manuscript twice. As a result he had numerous comments and I believe all of them resulted in changes.

Various friends of the Welch family also came forth with information along with Peter Welch, George's nephew. John Norbert of Purdue University whose book, "Wings of their Dreams: Purdue in Flight," includes material on George Welch, filled in the blanks about George's time there before joining the Army Air Corps. The admissions office at St. Andrews, Welch's prep school, confirmed his time as a student there.

Karla Niemann, an assistant to U.S. Sen. James Inhofe (R-OK) has been helpful, especially in my efforts to get Ken and George upgraded to the Congressional Medal of Honor.

I also wish to thank Col. George Farfour USAF for his research on Ken Taylor; Steve Diamond, one of the military historians in Hawaii and my nephew, retired U.S. Amb. Curtis Struble for pointing me to necessary changes.

Table of Contents

Foreword

Seventy years have passed since the Japanese attack on Pearl Harbor. And there has been no dearth of books written about the attack. However, ironically, the story of the U. S. Army Air Corps has been neglected. Most of the books about the Pearl Harbor attack have been written about the attack itself, the personalities involved, the strategy and the blame game—who was responsible for the American disaster. In this book the author, John Martin Meek, attempts to bring to the reader an expanded story of the U. S. Army Air Corps on that famous day of infamy.

While he describes the role of the Army Air Corps, which he claims was responsible for shooting down a dozen of the 353 Japanese planes in the attack, he concentrates on two pilots of the 47th Pursuit Squadron, 2nd Lts. Ken Taylor and George Welch, who are officially credited with six planes and maybe more. In essence this is the story of these two men

Spending more than ten years of his life with painstaking research talking with the families, friends, men of the 47th Pursuit Squadron and Ken Taylor himself, Meek portrays the life of the two pilots from Nov. 30 to Dec. 6 and concludes with their actions on Dec. 7.

An underlying theme running throughout this book is how poorly records in those days were kept and how it was almost impossible to recreate what happened that day. The author concludes because of the lack of records and witnesses many at Pearl Harbor including Taylor and Welch deserved more recognition but have never received it.

By telling this story. he hopes to get these men upgraded from the Distinguished Service Cross to the Congressional Medal of Honor, highest medal in the land for bravery, but because of the lack of witnesses and records he has been so far unable to do so. While the book lacks footnotes and sources there is an excellent bibliography which can help those interested delve into this story more deeply.

This is an entertaining read that I believe is an important work because it adds to the Pearl Harbor literature a missing dimension—the story of two men who are usually given only one or two lines in most books but were truly American heroes and who, unlike many on that fateful morning, were not asleep.

—Donald M. Goldstein Ph.D
Professor Emeritus University Of Pittsburgh
Co-author of *At Dawn We Slept: the Untold Story of Pearl Harbor, God's Samurai: Lead Pilot at Pearl Harbor* and *Dec. 7, 1941: The Day the Japanese Attacked Pearl Harbor.*

Prologue

"All the publicity is 'Remember Pearl Harbor.' They should take a look at Hickam Field or what was Hickam Field. Twenty-seven bombs hit the main barracks. They dropped about 100 bombs on Hickam, practically all hits. The papers say they are poor bombardiers! They were perfect on nearly all their releases."

—Maj. Charles P. Eckhert, Army Air Forces, "7 December 1941 The Air Force Story," p. 59.

No military event in American history surpasses the surprise attack by Japanese forces at dawn on Dec. 7, 1941 on mostly U.S. military facilities at various locations on the island of Oahu, then the Territory of Hawaii.

It was an enormous and potentially brilliant maneuver by the Imperial Japanese military forces to destroy the U.S. Navy fleet in the Pacific in one great swoop, thus assuring Japan of continued success in adding to already impressive conquests in the South Pacific and Far East.

The naval task force assembled by Fleet Adm. Isoruku Yamamoto almost avoided any detection warning U.S.

Forces on the island of Oahu in Hawaii, so they could mount a major defense against some 350 Japanese fighters and bombers assembled in an armada of 57 ships including six aircraft carriers. Each Japanese aircraft was given specific targets to attack or other strategic assignments over Oahu.

In "God's Samurai," the story of Mitsuo Fuchida, who led the Japanese attack on Dec. 7, 1941, Gordon W. Prange, Donald M. Goldstein and Katherine V. Dillon, the authors, wrote "On the voyage to Hawaii, Fuchida found plenty to occupy his mind. He kept his airmen busy studying mock-ups of Pearl Harbor and Oahu, along with models of American warships, going over every angle of the tactics again and again until each man's part became second nature to him."

Brilliant as this bold action appeared to those commanding the massive Japanese war machine, its leaders such as Prime Minister Tojo and Adm. Yamamoto apparently did not see the many flaws in its planning and execution.

For example, while eight of the U.S. Navy battleships were anchored in Pearl Harbor at the time, not a single one of the seven U.S. aircraft carriers was in that port during the attack. The Enterprise, Lexington and Saratoga were assigned to the Pacific while the Yorktown, Hornet, Wasp and Ranger were in the Atlantic.

By then, both the Japanese military operating in the Far East and Hitler's Nazi forces in Europe fully understood the significance of air power in their previous, current and future military successes.

In spite of the leadership of Gen. Billy Mitchell and others to instill air power as a major factor in U.S. military operations, at the time of Pearl Harbor it was still a hard sell.

As the late B. Gen. Kenneth M. Taylor USAF Ret. said in an interview Nov. 19, 2001, the Army Air Corps when he was in flight school in 1940–41 was not enthusiastic about training pilots, and made it as difficult as possible for flying cadets to earn their wings.

On reflection it seems unimaginable that the U.S. military leaders, especially those with the responsibility for our forces in Hawaii, had no real plans in operation for a defense against an aerial attack by the Japanese.

This lack of preparation was at virtually all levels from a major, easily executed strategic plan for the defense of Hawaii's military bases to not having all forces on alert considering the crisis in diplomatic affairs at that specific time between the U.S. and Japan.

The unfortunate circumstances of Dec. 7, 1941, and there were many, had their déjà vu 60 years later on Sept. 11, 2001 when a group of Islamic terrorists decided to fly hijacked U.S. airliners into the World Trade Center buildings in New York, the Pentagon and probably one other target in Washington, DC. As in 1941 in Hawaii, the massive U.S. military forces had no operative plan for downing threats from hijacked airliners before they reached their targets including the Pentagon along with the World Trade Towers.

The consequences were that instead of a small number of passengers on the airliners being killed had U.S. fighter aircraft been able to scramble and shoot them down before they reached their targets (as it happened, all aboard the airliners perished when the planes crashed) the loss of lives ended up being almost 600 more than those who perished on Dec. 7, 1941.

In both instances, not surprisingly there was a rush to fix the blame instead of fixing the problem.

Soon after the attack on Hawaii, the two top military commanders, Navy Adm. Husband Kimmel and Army Lt. Gen. Walter Short, were relieved of their commands for lack of leadership in not having been better prepared for defending the island and its military facilities.

As the 70th anniversary of the Pearl Harbor attack approaches, the debate continues on whether some intelligence about the Japanese plan of attack was withheld from or not sent to Kimmel and Short as both commanders insisted had occurred.

But considering the successes of the Japanese war machine and the widely known exigency in diplomatic relations between the U.S. and Japan, the case easily can be made that common sense preparations ordered by Kimmel and Short should have transcended lack of intelligence sharing.

In fact the most recent investigation of Pearl Harbor, the 1995 Dorn Report by the U.S. Department of Defense, arrives at that conclusion.

On Dec. 7, 1999, the Navy Historical Foundation held a symposium at the Navy Memorial in Washington, DC about the blame placed on Adm. Kimmel for not having had the vessels and forces in his command prepared for an enemy aerial attack.

The format was two speakers supporting Kimmel and two giving reasons why he was to blame.

A speaker defending Kimmel was the late Capt. Ed Beach USN Ret., the veteran submariner and distinguished author of fourteen books including "Run Silent, Run Deep."

Capt. Beach pointed out that in addition to a lack of good communications between the Navy Department in Washington, DC and Adm. Kimmel's command in Hawaii, both the antiaircraft weapons and ammo on several ships were outmoded and in the process of being updated at the time.

But Capt. Beach also suggested in his remarks that considering the overwhelming Japanese forces attacking Hawaii, having had the U.S. military on high alert would have resulted in somewhat the same outcome.

He said that even if Adm. Kimmel had known the attack was going to happen, his Navy antiaircraft guns would not have brought down many more Japanese planes.

In his talk, Capt. Beach did not bother to mention the mission of the Army Air Corps pursuit squadrons there to protect the fleet in Pearl Harbor, and what they did do and what more they might have done if on alert in the aerial defense against the Japanese attackers.

Capt. Beach's views are certainly debatable. Take one example. Even with no U.S. unit on alert for an aerial attack, no Navy ships at general quarters and no fighter aircraft in the air when the Japanese arrived over Hawaii, through a combination of ground fire and aerial combat almost ten percent of the Yamamoto's aircraft were downed that day.

Had all gunners been in position and all fighter aircraft in the air, Gen. Ken Taylor said in his Nov. 19, 2001 interview, "We would have made them pay."

Just as with the terrorist acts on 9/11, the few visionaries who foresaw Hawaii being attacked by the Japanese were ignored.

In that situation fault for lack of preparedness should not be placed solely with President Roosevelt as commander-in-chief and the U.S. military forces.

Back then Congress and the country were in an isolationist mood, very much against getting involved in Hitler's dangerous conquests in Europe and what Japan was doing in the Far East.

The extension of the military draft, for example, had passed Congress by only one vote in the summer of 1941, and America did not want to enter another terrible world war slightly more than two decades after the end of World War I–"the war to end all wars" it was thought.

We now know Roosevelt had heeded the pleas of Great Britain's Winston Churchill for aid in defending against the Nazi dreadnaught. Some of what FDR was doing to help England was known to the public, much of it was going on in secret.

Years before Pearl Harbor, wars raged in the Far East with Japan's aggression and Hitler's numerous successful conquests in Europe and Africa. Yet America ostensibly was doing nothing.

And the Pearl Harbor attack was not the first act of aggression by a foreign power against the United States in 1941.

On Oct. 31, the U.S.S. Reuben James DD245 was torpedoed and sunk by U-552, a German submarine as it was escorting merchant ships going to the aid of Britain in the vicinity of Iceland. We lost 115 Navy men (44 survived) but war was not declared against Germany.

Whether or not Adm. Yamamoto, who had spent time in his country's diplomatic service in America, actually predicted the Pearl Harbor attack "would awaken a sleeping giant," as the actor who plays him in "Tora! Tora! Tora!" says, it certainly did.

Congress declared war the next day retroactive to Dec. 7, and Americans by the thousands rushed to military recruiting offices volunteering to serve.

America burst into a frenzy of patriotism. In time millions of men were mobilized for the armed services and women in uniform served in such duties as ferrying aircraft to combat zones, nursing and clerical work.

Industry retooled to make aircraft, land weapons and other military equipment, rations on many consumer goods were initiated and shortly a giant American war machine was in place.

Even as President George W. Bush tends to be solely blamed by the media and millions of Americans for starting the war in Iraq, we are inclined to forget that in our Constitutional system the president *proposes* and the Congress *disposes*.

While the 2008 presidential campaign was producing a new leader for our country, among Democrats in the race there was much debate about the wisdom of the U.S. senators who voted to support President Bush's plan to invade Iraq and those who opposed it.

In other historical events such as the concept of continuing the Vietnam and Iraq wars, we apparently will forever debate who's to be blessed and who's to be blamed for the tragedy of Dec. 7, 1941.

For the Pearl Harbor attack, there are many to blame and few to bless.

No specific advanced warning was given the military, our forces were not on alert nor was there any system in place as to what the various military units were to do even if forewarned an attack was imminent.

As the sky over Oahu filled with Japanese war birds, those U.S. armed forces not killed or severely wounded by the first bullets and bombs did their best to quickly act as they had been trained.

This was most difficult at Pearl Harbor where 178 Navy vessels including eight battleships were anchored or were within three miles of Oahu with none on the alert for a possible attack.

In a short period of time most of the battleships were capsized, sunk or badly damaged. Those sailors and marines who were able to abandon ship found themselves in a harbor where the water was burning with oil leaking from the damaged vessels. Many were trapped below decks never to escape and others perished from the bombs and strafing of the Japanese aircraft.

It was a near total devastation of the Navy's proud Pacific Fleet. The one major flaw in Adm. Yamamoto's strategy was that the Navy's carriers were scattered here and there and none in port at Pearl when the attack came.

These absent carriers proved to be a major factor in Japan's eventual defeat from carrying the Doolittle Raiders to bomb Tokyo to destroying much of the Japanese Navy in the Battle of Midway.

So what was the other Pearl Harbor?

The primary post-attack focus on Pearl Harbor itself and not all the military installations in Hawaii hit by the Japanese attack harked back to Feb. 15, 1898 when the U.S.S. Maine exploded and sank in the harbor at Havana, Cuba.

This incident sparked the beginning of the Spanish-American War shortly thereafter.

But almost instantly a cry rang out across America expressing the shock of the sinking of one of this country's first battleships. It was, "Remember the Maine." Actually, forgotten over the years was the full epitaph, "Remember the Maine, To Hell with Spain."

Not long after the attack on Pearl Harbor as patriotism exploded to a crescendo across the nation, we had a new rallying cry–"Remember Pearl Harbor."

Most Americans had no idea where Pearl Harbor was located when the news of the attack first reached the mainland, and from the beginning the media's reporting was on the damage to the Navy's Pacific Fleet and not what had happened to other military facilities on the island such as the destruction of most of the Air Corps planes at Wheeler Field.

And plenty had happened to the Army at its bases there.

With Adm. Yamamoto's strategy of first taking out the Army Air Corps planes whose primary mission was to protect the fleet at anchor, the devastation of Army bases came near equaling the mayhem at Pearl.

The major difference was that the war vessels in Pearl Harbor were anchored in an area not much larger than one or two square miles, whereas the Army's facilities were scattered from one side of the island to the other—an area of 607 square miles. (Navy and Marine airfields were in different areas on the island but none was able to get a plane airborne to oppose the attackers.)

Hickam Field, for example, was down near Pearl Harbor. Schofield Barracks and Wheeler were almost dead center on Oahu. Bellows Field was off near the shore to the island's southeast and Haleiwa was on the North Shore. For some reason, probably because it was an auxiliary field, Haleiwa was strafed by only one enemy plane.

The number of men who went down with the U.S.S. Arizona and those killed on other ships such as the U.S.S. Oklahoma has become in the decades since almost exclusively the story of what happened on Dec. 7.

Even today documentaries such as The History Channel's two-disc DVD set on the Pearl Harbor attack and the National Geographic's six-disc documentary on World War II focus exclusively on what happened to the Navy at Pearl Harbor. This kind of presentation has questionable credibility as a comprehensive recounting of "the date which will live in infamy."

The Army suffered greatly both with hundreds of dead and wounded and at all the airfields except Haleiwa the barracks, mess halls, hangars, most of the aircraft, storage facilities and even homes and non-military vehicles were damaged or destroyed.

There are two significant exceptions to the mostly Pearl Harbor portrayal of the events of Dec. 7. Both are films.

The first was the 1970 Twentieth Century-Fox production, "Tora! Tora! Tora!," which presented the story of the attack from both the American and Japanese sides.

Almost four decades later this film is considered a World War II classic where the story was told with some typical Hollywood variations but is a fairly accurate picture of what happened. Next came the 2001 Touchstone Pictures production, "Pearl Harbor," directed by Jerry Bruckheimer, one of the contemporary titans of the film and television industry.

"Pearl Harbor" was told mainly through the characters of two Air Corps pilots who variously not only were heroes of the Dec. 7, 1941 attack but also fought with the RAF and went on the Doolittle Raid to Tokyo.

One reviewer cynically wrote at the time that the film "was almost as destructive as Pearl Harbor."

While the bombs hitting on the land military facilities were no less effective than at Pearl, many Army, Navy, Marine and Coast Guard personnel were able to scramble to safety against roadside curbs, in ditches and other shelters.

Even though the mission of the Army Air Corps in Hawaii was to protect the Navy fleet, none of its units was on alert to execute either an air or ground defense against an air attack with antiaircraft and machine guns.

But, as with the Navy, Army officers and enlisted men did what they could to fight back, put out fires and care for the wounded.

Amazingly, several pilots from different Army Air Corps units were able to get into the air to shoot down some of the Japanese planes. In all, historians now believe from both U.S. and Japanese records a total of 29 enemy planes out of 350 (a figure not consistent in various historical narratives) were downed either by aerial combat or ground fire.

But gradually over the years since Dec. 7, 1941 the vast destruction and loss of lives at the various Army facilities unfortunately have fallen by the wayside in accounts of the tragedy.

Among the Air Corps pilots who were able to get airborne that morning were two second lieutenants only a few months out of flight school with shiny gold bars and silver wings on their uniforms.

While young and inexperienced, both had taken their training seriously and after arriving in Hawaii quickly were named to head two flights in the newly activated 47th Pursuit Squadron based at Wheeler Field.

The pilots were 2nd Lts. Kenneth M. Taylor of Hominy, Oklahoma and George S. Welch of Wilmington, Delaware.

While one was a country boy and the other a city kid who had spent five years at an exclusive Delaware prep school, early on they bonded as buddies both on duty and partying around the island on Waikiki Beach and at the officers' clubs.

From the first minutes of the Japanese attack on Dec. 7, Taylor and Welch instantly switched from the weekend party mode to military discipline, taking to the air as two American planes against the huge number of aircraft sent by Yamamoto.

They are among the many heroes of that day except in their case Taylor and Welch within the week were designated by the U.S. War Department *as the first two heroes of World War II*, and would be awarded the Distinguished Service Cross—highest award given by the Army strictly for heroism in combat.

While both Taylor and Welch are mentioned in most books, documentaries and a movie about the Pearl Harbor attack, there are so many variations about what they did that day the objective of this narrative has been to get the story as straight as possible. In doing so the research has gone far beyond an interview with Gen. Taylor on Nov. 19, 2001 and many other conversations with him to other survivors of the 47th squadron and elsewhere—enriching this story with personal witnessing and insights not available in historical accounts to date.

Taylor and Welch, along with dozens of other heroes on Dec. 7, 1941, will forever have the blessings of Americans for what they did to carry out their oaths to protect and defend their country and without doubt prevented the deaths and injuries of numerous military personnel through their courageous action.

This is their story.

It is based on some forty years of friendship with Gen. and Mrs. Ken Taylor, the core piece being an hour-long interview done with him on Nov. 19, 2001 to have a record of what happened on Dec. 7, 1941 in his own words. From early 2000 until his death on Nov. 25, 2006, the Taylors were questioned many times to clear up conflicts and contradictions about what has been written and said (in books, movies and documentaries) via various accounts.

The material in this book also reflects thousands of hours of research over some nine years reaching from the National Archives in College Park, Maryland, to Haleiwa, Hawaii where Lts. Taylor and Welch roared off in the P-40s from a small Air Corps auxiliary field to take on an estimated 350 Japanese planes attacking U.S. military bases all over the island of Oahu that fateful morning.

Also during this time there were communications with Giles Welch, George Welch's son, and Peter Welch, his nephew. The material in the following chapters also represents two interviews and numerous email and phone conversations with Maj. Gen. Gordon Austin USAF Ret., commander of the Air Corps' 47th Pursuit Squadron at the time of the Pearl Harbor attack; conversations with Lt. Col. Kermit Tyler USAF Ret., operations officer on Dec. 7 and other Army survivors.

The eight chapters are written in the creative nonfiction style used by Truman Capote "In Cold Blood" and many other works of literature, reflecting the years of research on the Pearl Harbor project. Additional material can be found on the web site, www.pearlharborhero.net, produced in the fall of 2006 to honor Gen. Taylor and George Welch on the 65th anniversary of the Pearl Harbor attack.

November 30, 1941

"In late November, Col. (William J.) Flood, new
Wheeler Field commander, reported to Gen.
(Frederick) Martin's office, along with the other base
and tactical commanders, was briefed on a message
outlining the strained relations between the Japanese
and the United States, and instructed to implement
Alert One for sabotage. Earlier, earthen bunkers had
been built all around Wheeler for about 125 aircraft
so they would be suitably dispersed and protected
from air attack. Col. Flood asked if he could keep
the aircraft dispersed, but Gen. (Walter) Short dis-
approved his request. He therefore had all the aircraft
pulled in and parked together on the ramp, then increased the guards around the aircraft and around the
perimeter of the field."

—"7 December 1941 The Air Force Story," p. 48.

The windows of the new red Buick on the driver's and
passenger's sides were rolled down about half way, letting
the cool night air circulate through the vehicle.

The driver pushed in the clutch and shifted from third
to second gear to keep up speed with the gradual rise of

the road to higher ground. Both driver and passenger had lighted cigarettes, blowing the smoke out their mouths at times or through the nostrils with other puffs.

Both were dressed in formal attire but the driver before starting out had neatly folded his white dinner jacket and placed it on the back seat next to a pile of white silk that was the mess of an unfurled parachute.

"That was a really dumb thing you did tonight," said the driver.

"It got a big laugh and even some applause, mostly from the ladies," said the passenger, smiling proudly.

"There's probably some stupid regulation about behavior unbecoming an officer that could get you a court martial for that crazy stunt."

"I did see a Navy four-striper in his fancy little ice cream suit and gold braid, probably one of those Naval Academy boys, who was looking pissed. But nobody there except you knows my name. So how is he going to find out who did it among all the shave-tail Army second lieutenants here on the island? No way, Kenny boy."

"You wore a chute under your tux jacket and pulled the ripcord right in the middle of the Royal Hawaiian Hotel Ballroom. There was enough silk on the ballroom floor to make a dress for every gal there. And you think you'll get away with it?"

"Just about everybody laughed and some clapped their hands. I don't give a hoot what anybody thinks. I thought it would be a fun shocker and I did it. That's that."

"And you don't think somebody might just check out the chutes in the hangar and find one missing? How you planning on getting that sonofabitch back?"

"I know how to pack a chute, Grits. Learned it myself in basic in case I ever didn't trust those guys who do it for us. I'm too drunk tonight, but first thing in the morning it will be back in the hangar. Consider this, we're going for gunnery practice at Haleiwa Monday and I may need it."

"Yeah," said the driver, "with your mother just being out here on a visit and keeping you on a leash, you were feeling a little frisky tonight anyway.'

"You got that right," laughed the passenger. "Being Irish, my mom wanted to be assured the Army was taking good care of her baby boy. She even wanted to check out my room. I'm just sorry I didn't introduce her to Capt. Austin. That would have convinced her I'm in good hands."

A half hour later the Buick stopped at the guard gate at Wheeler Field. The corporal on duty saluted and came over to get a better look at the car's occupants.

"Lieutenants Taylor and Welch from the 47th squadron," said the driver.

"Yes sir," said the corporal, saluting again. "Good evening, sirs."

"That man needs a watch. What does he mean, 'Good evening?'" asked the driver. "Hell, a few more hours and it'll be time for breakfast."

"Why don't we stop at the club and have one more drink?" asked the passenger. "There'll be a poker game going on and if we can get in for a few hands, maybe win enough to go out on the town next Saturday night."

"Wheaties, we've both had too much to drink already. But I'm always up for a little poker. We can sleep in and go swimming at Waikiki tomorrow, work on our tans a little. Maybe meet some rich gals over here on vacation. What do you think?"

"Grits," said the passenger with a slight slur in his voice," I think it's just wonderful that you bought this car and we have some way to get around over here since I got grounded by that stupid cop for being drunk and making an illegal left turn in Honolulu. Hell, yes, I'm for hitting Waikiki tomorrow afternoon."

There were a few minutes of silence as the two headed from the Wheeler gate to the officer's club.

"By the way, Kenny boy, what happened to that cute blonde with the big southern accent you met a few weeks ago? Being from Oklahoma, didn't she know she was supposed to stop in California with all the other Okies?"

"Oh, George, we didn't hit it off too well," said the driver getting out of the Buick and slamming the door. "Her folks are divorced so she's out here visiting her old man who works at the shipyard or somewhere. Daddy's little girl no doubt and I'm momma's little boy so we ought to hit it off real good."

George was surprised. "Her parents are divorced?"

Ken shrugged, seeming unconcerned with the subject of their conversation.

"What was the strange name of that town in Oklahoma where she comes from?"

"Hennessey."

"Hennessey, oh, like the brandy."

"Wheaties, we don't know much about fancy drinks like brandy in Oklahoma. I don't know about Delaware, but our state is dry. Selling booze is against the law. Will Rogers, that actor from back there, said 'Oklahomans will keep voting for prohibition as long as they can stagger to the polls.'"

"Then how did you Acacia boys get your liquor for parties at the University of Oklahoma?"

"Bootleggers. Probably cheaper than in most states because when you get booze from a bootlegger there are no taxes involved. And, what's even better, they deliver it right to your door."

"Grits, you have a lot of towns in Oklahoma with names like Hennessey and Hominy?"

"Yes," said Taylor.

"Like what?"

"Oh," said Taylor, "we have the three hardest towns in Oklahoma."

"You mean," asked Welch, "oil towns and places like that with bar fights?"

"No, the three hardest towns in Oklahoma are Cement, Granite and Rocky."

"You're shitting me."

"Nope. And I can top that."

"Okay, Okie, have at it."

"Well, George, over in eastern Oklahoma we have a town called Maud and another one called Bowlegs. And the deal is from one direction you have to go through Bowlegs to get to Maud."

Welch laughed. "You're making this up like your having lived in a teepee."

"Nope, no bull about this. You don't believe me, just get yourself a map of Oklahoma and find out I'm not lying."

It was almost 2 a.m. and the club was empty except for a dark skinned bartender and four officers playing poker over in a corner. While George Welch, the passenger, went to the bar for two beers Ken Taylor, the driver, sauntered over to check out the game.

"Get out of here, Taylor," said one of the young officers, looking up. The four men playing cards also were dressed in tuxes, required for Saturday nights at Hawaii officers' clubs. Taylor had put his white dinner jacket back on.

"What the hell is your problem?" Taylor dragged up two chairs from another table and sat watching the action.

"I haven't forgotten how you cleaned me out just before we graduated from flight school at Brooks, and if you're getting in I'm getting out."

"Well," drawled Taylor, "as we say back in Oklahoma, you pays your money and you takes your choice."

Another officer was shuffling the cards. The one who had been talking to Taylor stood to leave.

"You can have my place, and I would suggest you guys staying in watch this Okie very closely. He's either got an ace up his sleeve, or somewhere else."

The players laughed and another one stood to leave.

"George, you can have my place. I've got to go to mass in the morning and it's getting a little late."

Taylor and Welch set their beers on the table and took the empty chairs.

"Deal 'em," said the Oklahoman.

"And preferably from the top," quipped Welch.

Both Taylor and Welch put their money on the table and picked up their cards.

"What are we playing here?" asked Taylor.

"Five-card stud," said one of the officers. "That okay with you guys?"

Both Taylor and Welch nodded and the game was underway. It continued for about an hour after Taylor had won several hands, then the four scattered for their quarters.

It was about 7 a.m. the next morning when Taylor was awakened by the loud engine noise of a low-flying airplane.

He rolled over in his bed at the Wheeler Officers' Club and realized he was more than just slightly hungover.

Those Navy sumbitches, he thought, *if they want to play the Sunday morning reveille game, one of these days I'm going to fly over their quarters so low they'll think I'm Santa coming down the chimney.*

He lay there for a few minutes then got out of bed wearing nothing but his olive drab boxer shorts.

Taylor was somewhat fastidious but the night before he had overdone the drinking and was so tired he had just slipped out of his tux and left it lying on a chair. After hanging it up in his little closet and washing up, he pulled on his khakis and headed down the hallway toward the screened in lanai at the end of the building. He stopped, stretched, yawned then walked over to the adjoining building where Welch had a room. He rapped on the door a few times.

"George," he called. "Might as well get up and join me for breakfast. Those Navy guys buzzing the field have ruined our sleeping in again and they're gonna pay for this I promise you that."

From inside his room Welch mumbled something about Taylor going ahead to the club and he would be there as soon as he could wake up and get dressed.

"I'll just grab a smoke and wait for you outside."

Shortly Welch appeared dressed in freshly laundered and starched khakis, the same uniform Taylor was wearing.

As the two young lieutenants made their way across the street to the club they were surprised to meet up with Lt. Rogers, the deputy commander and operations officer for their squadron.

Both Taylor and Welch saluted and greeted their superior officer, intending to keep going to the club.

"Morning, sir," drawled Taylor.

Oklahoma is a state where most people are somewhat laid back and usually friendly, so Taylor often was the first to speak when meeting up with someone.

"Lieutenants, come to attention," said their superior. "You know, sometimes I wonder how you were never taught the proper way to salute a fellow officer when you were in flight school. Things must be getting a lot looser since I went through flight training."

"Sir," said Welch, "I thought we did give you a proper salute."

Taylor and Welch even as young pilots knew Rogers, a first lieutenant, was a West Point graduate and their few months in flight school was nothing compared to his four years of rigid training to become an officer.

"Yes sir," said Taylor. "But it's Sunday morning and I said 'good morning' and I thought that courtesy seemed sufficient."

The senior officer was not amused either by Taylor's or Welch's responses, or the fact the former wasn't wearing a tie.

"Lieutenants," barked Rogers. "I've demonstrated to you at least twice the proper way to salute and it appears it was a waste of time. So go on to breakfast. And Taylor, when you finish eating return to your quarters and put on a tie. This is still the Army, not some Boy Scout camp."

"Yessir," said the two pilots simultaneously, saluting again and then turning to leave.

"Lieutenants, come to attention! I don't remember dismissing you."

They immediately brought their legs together with arms stiffly at the side, looking directly ahead at their superior.

"This is the United States Army of which you now are a member," snapped Rogers. "We obviously are on the verge of getting into a world war considering what's happening with Hitler in Germany and the Japanese land grabs all over Asia. Fighting wars takes discipline. There's no room for a lack of military manner when you're an officer in the U.S. Army. And you young shave-tails better understand that and understand it *right now*."

Rogers paused for a moment.

"I assume you know the squadron will be flying over to Haleiwa in the morning for gunnery practice. So we'll get an opportunity to see how our young hotshots do living in tents and going through chow lines as it is in the real Army. In fact, if I had my way I would leave you both over there for a month. Teach you that Army life is not just flying planes and partying on weekends."

"Well sir," said Taylor, still at attention, "I kinda look forward to gunnery practice, and since I grew up in a tee-pee back in Oklahoma those tents with cots will be kind of a luxury."

Lt. Rogers was no dummy. His face reddened at the smartass attitude of the young second lieutenant and what he had just said.

But, before he could begin a new dressing down of Taylor for his comment about sleeping in a teepee Rogers remembered one of the senior officers in the Army Air Corps was B. Gen. Clarence Tinker, a renowned Osage Indian from Oklahoma who was the first Native American to reach the rank of general.

Welch almost choked to keep from laughing at the audacity of Taylor's lie. While Taylor, given the nickname "Grits" by Welch because he came from a town named Hominy, hadn't grown up in a big city such as Wilmington, Delaware where his father worked for DuPont, Welch knew his buddy had been a frat boy back at the University of Oklahoma and was no country yokel.

"The dining room will be closing soon," said Lt. Rogers. "I don't want you to miss your last breakfast in comfort for a couple of weeks, so you're dismissed."

Both pilots tried to give their best salute and walked toward the club.

"Who the hell licked the red off his lollypop?" said Taylor, not really that much upset by the West Pointer's lecture on military decorum.

"I've been listening to the news on the radio and what's going on with the Japs," he said, "and it seems like to me we should be up there in our planes ready to fight instead of farting around down here trying to have the perfect salute."

Just inside, Welch took off his officer's hat and slapped Taylor hard on the back.

"You lying sonofabitch! I bet you never saw a teepee in your whole life. I can't believe you could stand there with a straight face and pull that off."

"My old man used to be a gambler," said Taylor. "You get in a card game, you better know how to fake it which, by the way, is the reason you always lose at cards."

Both got in line for breakfast servings, the aroma of sausage, bacon and ham frying along with the burned smell of toasted bread filling the club dining room. Welch took a generous helping of scrambled eggs, ham, potatoes and toast. Taylor, always a little finicky about his food, waited for eggs over easy to go with his bacon and toast. When he joined George at the table he looked unhappy.

"I guess they never heard about biscuits in this Army," Taylor said, sitting opposite Welch at the table.

"What are biscuits?"

"They are those little round fluffy things that are served at breakfast at every home in Oklahoma every morning. Sometimes with butter and jelly. Sometimes with red-eye or cream gravy. Either way, good eats."

"Aren't grits mandatory back there?" asked Welch. "That kind of white, breakfast cereal stuff made out of corn?"

"Grits are not Oklahoma," said Taylor. "We are not the South in Oklahoma, we are in the Southwest. And we sometimes like a little chili with our biscuits."

"So what are you going to eat when we get to England besides tea and crumpets?"

"I've been thinking about that," responded Taylor. "There's nothing good I ever heard about grub in England, but then I've never actually known anyone who has ever been across the pond."

Welch picked up his mug of black coffee.

"We're going there, you know that?"

"I can't wait," said Taylor. "I didn't join the Air Corps to just be playing games in the air with other pilots and shooting at flag targets. And besides, as nice as it is here there must be more available women in England than Honolulu. Of course, once we're over there we'll be like the cavalry coming to the rescue of the Brits and the ladies will love us."

"You know Roosevelt is not going to do nothing and just let Hitler and the Germans invade England?"

"I reckon you're right, George. But when we get there we're going to be up against squadrons of Red Barons. The Kraut pilots have taken on the flyboys of all those countries Germany has run over and kicked their butts. If and when we get over there, I hope the Air Corps has enough gumption to let those Brit RAF pilots teach us a few tricks. Since we've been in Hawaii out of flight school both of us have doubled our hours in the air from 200 to 400, but that's not the same as taking on pilots who have knocked off enemy planes all over Europe."

"This is a strange conversation," said Welch. "Here we are in the middle of the Pacific not so far from where the Japs probably have conquered as much or more territory than the Nazis, and we're not even thinking about all the experience those meatball pilots have under their belts."

Both had finished their breakfasts and were sipping on the refill of black coffee.

"There's a rumor going around," said Taylor, "that the big brass had a briefing the other day about the way things are going with the Japs. I'm guessing we will be sent to England, but there's a very good chance we might get into a war with Japan and end up in the Philippines or somewhere out there pretty soon. About a third of my class at Brooks went out to the Philippines and it would be good to fly with them again."

"I'm not afraid of taking on Jap pilots," Welch declared.

"Why not? You think our training out here has really prepared us for those guys who, just like the Krauts, probably have more time in combat than we have in our log books?"

Welch took a final gulp of coffee and was getting up to leave.

"Either way, Grits, whether it's England or out here on some God forsaken island, it's going to be tough. And it's Roosevelt and the politicians back in Washington who are going to decide where we fight and our role will just be as cannon fodder."

Both pilots laughed as Welch grabbed his hat and they headed for the door. With no duty for the day, there was little reason not to head back to their quarters for more sleep.

The sun was bright as they left the club and looked at the hangars and other buildings that made up Wheeler Field, resting in the middle of a vast area of dark green grass.

Outside, Welch suddenly snapped the fingers of one hand.

"Damn."

"What's wrong, Wheaties? Forget something?"

"Yeah," said Welch. "I've got to grab that chute in your Buick, get over to the chute storage area and get it packed again. And now that I'm sober, Grits, you're right. Opening that up on the dance floor was a stupid thing to do."

"It's done now."

"Yeah," Welch responded. "I just hope that Navy Mr. Ice Cream Suit doesn't play Sherlock Holmes and try to track me down."

Waving goodbye to his buddy, he headed for for Taylor's car to get the chute.

Current events of that day: *Packers beat the Redskins. The U.S.S. Woodworth, a new destroyer, was launched in San Francisco. Ramona and Mercedes Spencer, riding bikes, were struck by a car and Frank Rosado, 41, died in Honolulu. FDR's train hurried back to Washington, DC. from Warm Springs, GA, for him to confer with Secretary of State Hull on the Orient crisis. The Russians recaptured Rostov from the Nazis. A threat to Thailand seen as Japan Army masses. Li'l Abner's rich Aunt Bessie decides to entertain Princess No-No of Rhumboogie in the comics.*

December 1, 1941

"Intense training became a way of life for the pilots.
Lieutenant Sanders, who had been appointed commander of the 46th Squadron, cautioned his men to
'Learn something every time you fly. There's a war
coming on. I don't know just when, but knowing
what you're doing is your life insurance.'"
—"7 December 1941 The Air Force Story," p. 44.

It was 8 a.m. and with bellies full of breakfast the pilots of
the 47th Pursuit Squadron wearing flight suits were assem-
bling in Hangar No. 2 at Wheeler Field to sit in metal
folding chairs for a briefing.

Wheeler, being higher and near the center of the
Island of Oahu, was somewhat different from the traditional airfields such as Hickam and Bellows being nearer
the water. The vast grass area of the Wheeler Field area
away from housing, hangars, recreation areas and other
buildings made it look more like an industrial park rather
than a military base.

Honoring the memory of Maj. Sheldon H. Wheeler, a
former commander of Luke Field on Ford Island in Pearl

Harbor and victim of a July 13, 1921 plane crash, it had been officially designated Wheeler Field on Nov. 11, 1922 only a few months after a team headed by Lt. William Agee had arrived at Schofield Barracks to build the facility.

On the walk over from breakfast at the Officers' Club Taylor stopped to have an after breakfast smoke, taking a green and red pack of Lucky Strikes from his flight suit. Welch was walking a few steps behind him taking drags on a Camel.

Before entering the hangar all cigarettes were field stripped as the pilots slowly settled into chairs.

Standing idly by waiting for everyone to be seated were Capt. Gordon Austin, the squadron commander, and 1st.Lt. Bob Rogers, operations officer and second in command.

Austin was a tall, handsome man, West Point class of 1936. In the peacetime Army promotions were earned the hard way. Both Austin and Rogers not only had abundant experience, but exceptional leadership qualities to have reached the rank of captain and first lieutenant.

Privately, Col. Flood, the Wheeler Field commander, had told Austin he was being promoted to major but the paperwork had not yet cleared to make it official.

"Attention!" yelled Rogers, his voice echoing throughout the hangar.

All the pilots arose, arms at their sides and everyone facing forward.

"This is a very important week for this squadron," said Rogers. "Capt. Austin will now give the briefing. At ease!"

The pilots sat down and the squadron commander stepped forward, his height of six feet three inches was somewhat above that of most of the young men sitting before him. With his feet wide apart and his hands behind his back Capt. Austin began the briefing.

"This week, gentlemen" he began, "we are moving out to Haleiwa for gunnery practice. This auxiliary field as most of you know is about ten miles away over on the North Shore.

"The runway out there is not the same as Wheeler. It stretches from the beach way back into some trees where the tents and other facilities are located.

"The runway looks kind of like honeycomb and is called pierced steel planking or PSP, and fits together with interlocking strips. So it may take a few takeoffs and landings to get used to it.

"There's a little town up there with a bar and movie theater and that's about it. If you can make some arrangement to get your cars out there, for those of you who have one, I expect most evenings will be free if you want to come back here to the club. But we will be eating and sleeping at the strip. The road between here and Haleiwa isn't much, so be careful when you're driving it.

"About a week ago," and Austin paused for a moment, "the military high command out here held a briefing about the very major crisis existing between our country and Japan. Diplomatically events are not going well between us and the Japs."

Austin paused again and began looking his pilots straight in the eye.

"As of today" he continued, "my guess is we shortly will be on our way to the Philippines fighting the Japs.

Or some could be sent to the Philippines and some to England. And if we can come even close to holding our own against the Luftwaffe as the Royal Air Force pilots are doing, we will make our country proud.

"But, while Japan is thousands of miles away there is the distinct possibility we could be sent to Wake or Midway islands, the Philippines or somewhere out there to reinforce our men. If we go to war with Japan, there's no telling where it will start."

The captain relaxed, stepping forward toward his young charges.

"Go back to your quarters and get whatever gear you'll be needing at Haleiwa for the next two weeks. We will be living in tents. There will be an officer's country and club, but the mess will be in a line with the enlisted men. And if I hear of anybody pulling rank out there, you're going to have me to deal with later on.

"Now, go get your gear and let's get on with it. Lt. Rogers and I will lead the squadron out of Wheeler with a takeoff time of 0900 hours."

Rogers stepped forward. "Dismissed!"

Taylor sidled up to Welch as they headed back to their quarters in buildings just across the street from each other.

"I'm really looking forward to this," said Taylor. "About damned time we got out there."

"Well," smirked Welch, "oh great Indian chief, you're not going to have your own teepee you know. And there ain't going to be any young squaws waiting on you like back in Oklahoma."

"George, most of this gang has never ever pushed that button on the stick of a P-40 and heard the sound of their guns firing. I don't know what kind of flag targets they're going to have for us, but I'm going to shoot the shit out of whatever they put up."

At 0900 all the 47th pilots were in their P-40s with engines idling waiting for Capt. Austin and Lt. Rogers to take off so the others could follow.

Wheeler was different from most Army Air Corps fields with specific, hard surface runways where it was necessary to taxi to one end to begin takeoffs.

The field had a ramp area but much of the base was green grass amply watered by the frequent rains more than eight hundred feet above the sea level down in Honolulu. Outside the complex of hangars, the mess hall, barracks and other buildings there was plenty of room for the P-40s, P-36s and other aircraft to take off and land not being on the runway.

With an eye on the tall windsock, all pilots had to do was be sure nothing was in front of them and give their planes full throttle to get into the air.

Once airborne, Austin and Rogers circled at about three thousand feet until all the squadron was up then let them get into a "vee" formation heading into the very brief flight toward the North Shore and the auxiliary field.

The squadron flew on past Haleiwa and out to sea to give the pilots a feel of the air currents before landing on the little makeshift strip.

"Attention, 47th pilots," Capt. Austin's voice came over their radios. "Lt. Rogers and I are going down to 2000 feet to circle while you land. The right side of the 'vee' for both flights will land in the order in which you are now flying, followed by the left side. So go on down, boys."

The 47th had two flight leaders, Taylor and Welch.

Welch was the senior of the two having completed flight school a few months earlier than Taylor, joining the 47th in January. Taylor had showed up in May after getting his wings April 25 at Brooks Field near San Antonio.

It did not take long for Austin and Rogers observing Taylor and Welch to recognize they clearly were the top two pilots in the squadron and by summer had been designated as flight leaders.

Both were as one with their P-40s once they climbed into the cockpits.

"You know, Wheaties," Taylor told Welch one day, "there is just some wonderful, kind of sweet smell about being in a plane. Guess it's a mixture of the aviation fuel and other stuff in there but it's an aroma second only to a beautiful woman's perfume."

Taylor was the first to land at Haleiwa, and turned his plane to taxi back down the side of the strip toward the group of tents back under the trees not far from the ocean. Soon all the squadron's aircraft were on the ground and directed to the designated parking spots on the ramp by ground crews.

Once all the planes were down, the squadron's pilots sauntered up to the headquarters tent where Capt. Austin and Lt. Rogers were waiting, each pilot carrying the standard B-1 bag of toilet articles, clothes and other gear they would need for up to two weeks at Haleiwa.

"ATTENTION!" called out the Lt. Rogers.

The pilots dropped their gear and stood as ordered.

Austin stepped forward, always a little less military and more at ease than his subordinate.

"At ease. The ground crews will show you to your quarters, the mess tent and other facilities," said Austin. "Take your time in getting organized for living here for awhile, then report back at 1300 hours sharp for the briefing on gunnery practice."

A little warily Austin paused for a moment, looking over the group.

"Taylor and Welch stay here for a meeting on the procedures for their flights. For the rest of you, dismissed."

It was dark inside the tent, which consisted of three simple wooden desks, and a small conference table. At a smaller desk a corporal dressed in khakis and a "pisscutter" cap sat by a phone sorting papers.

"Sit down, boys," said Austin and all found chairs around the table.

"Look, lieutenants, I personally think we are going to be in a war very soon," he began. "Some of our pilots are just not ready to take on anything short of a Piper Cub. We've worked hard to get everybody ready not just to defend themselves, but to do a lot of damage to the enemy in aerial combat, strafing and whatever else we're assigned to do and come back in one piece."

He stopped to light a Chesterfield cigarette with the other three already smoking.

"It's no secret the Army hasn't yet figured out what Billy Mitchell tried to and did prove about air power.

They just don't see the great difference between what our boys in France were flying and what planes like our P-40s and B-17s can do today that Eddie Rickenbacker, the great World War I ace, never dreamed of.

"So, we're counting on you to see that the pilots in your flights make the most of our two weeks or so out here. This is not a time to be covering some buddy's ass. It's a time for kicking his ass to get this squadron ready to take on enemy pilots who can fly circles around us. Understand?"

"Yessir!" said Taylor and Welch in unison.

The four men stood and the two young pilots saluted, and then left the tent to pick up their bags and try to find their quarters.

"What do you think of our chances of getting a poker game going out here this week?" mused Taylor as they walked along. "I didn't win enough Saturday night to do much damage when we go out next weekend."

"Hell," responded Welch with humorous sarcasm. "It wouldn't matter if you won a hundred dollars. You'll never spend five bucks any night when you got a sucker like me picking up the tabs."

At 1300 hours all the pilots were back in front of the headquarters tent, where the two flights split up and went off to squat under the shade of P-40 wings to listen to what Taylor and Welch had to tell them about a revised plan for the afternoon.

It had developed that while the 47th squadron was in place as ordered, red tape back at Wheeler Field had delayed arrangements for the aircraft pulling the flag target for gunnery practice to be in the air. So Capt. Austin told Taylor and Welch to take their flights up, get into the standard "vee" formation and fly around the island so they would know the location of every major military facility such as Hickam Field, Schofield Barracks, Bellows Field, the docking area for Navy ships at Pearl Harbor and the Navy and Marine facilities at Ewa, Barbers Point and the Kaneohe Navy and Marine air stations.

"Sir," said Taylor, obviously annoyed they were not getting on with gunnery practice, "I think Welch and I and our boys pretty well know those locations by now. I've been out here eight months and George almost a year."

Austin was a patient man, not unused to dealing with smartass, shave-tail new officers with their little gold bars that metaphorically made some think their ideas also were golden.

"Lieutenant, I know how long both of you have been with my squadron," said Austin, annoyed by Taylor's attitude.

"I have no idea what you boys know about baseball. But in the spring every year, most of the major league teams go down to Florida for something called 'spring training.'

"Do you know why these clubs go to spring training? It's because even Lou Gehrig, Joe DiMaggio and the other major league players between seasons actually forget some of the basics of the game.

"Right now the assignment for Army Air Corps fighter squadrons out here in Hawaii is to defend the Navy fleet anchored at Pearl Harbor.

"We have been given initial points at various sites on Oahu. Able is Kahuku. Baker is Ulupppau, Koko Head is Cast, Pearl Harbor is Dog, Barber's Point is Easy, Lualualei is Fox, Kaena Point is George and Haleiwa is Hypo.

"William is Wheeler Field and Robert is the Interceptor Center and so forth.

"Every pilot in this squadron needs to know these basics, and I have the feeling they don't know them and don't always know where they are in the air over Oahu. After all, gentlemen, every day in Hawaii is not perfectly cloudless and sunny. We probably get more rain here than in almost anywhere on the mainland. And there may be some slight distractions when attacking aircraft are shooting at you. We need to be ready for every kind of situation, so regardless of circumstances we know every bit of this island like the palm of our hand. So you boys get in the air and make good use of the time this afternoon. Understood?"

As the two flight leaders saluted, left the tent and walked away, Welch snickered. Jabbing Taylor in his ribs with an elbow, Welch could not resist also giving his buddy a verbal prod.

"And another thing, Grits, you really ought to spend some time studying the pockets on a pool table so you know where the eight-ball goes, since you're not yet the Willy Hoppe of that game."

From what others could see, in spite of one being from a small rural town and the other from a sizable city, Taylor and Welch were something like a saying of that time, "two peas in a pod."

The only apparent characteristic they seemed to share was both were smaller men, which was typical of pilots with Capt. Austin and Lt. Rogers being exceptions.

Welch had been reared in an upper middle-class home in a sizable city, Wilmington, Delaware.

Born in 1919 just after World War I ended, his father's birth name was Schwartz. Because of the animosity that had developed against the Germans in America during World War I, the family took the mother's maiden name, Welch, and the youngest son became George Schwartz Welch.

At some point during his studies at the elite St. Andrews prep school in Middletown, Delaware he had decided to be an engineer and was advised by one of his teachers to go to Purdue in West Lafayette, Indiana, a university developing a specialty in aviation.

Welch joined the ROTC at Purdue, began studying mechanical engineering and pledged Delta Epsilon Fraternity. Having applied to be an Army Air Corps cadet, at the end of the fall semester in 1939 his application was accepted.

He was a handsome man with sharp facial features, a lop-sided smile and a strong propensity for pranks such as wearing the parachute under his dinner jacket the previous Saturday evening at the Royal Hawaiian Hotel dance.

Much of Welch's pleasure came from needling Taylor who, in his dry, Southwestern way, had no problem dodging Welch's verbal darts and giving back in kind.

Taylor also was an attractive young man, having just turned twenty-two at the time, with lighter hair compared to Welch's dark locks and memorable for something of a frequent smirk on his face as if he had a great secret known to no one but himself.

He was born in Enid, Oklahoma, in the northern part of the state but grew up in Hominy after his parents, the Joe Taylors, moved to the little community closer to Tulsa.

Times were still hard in the Sooner State when Taylor graduated from high school in 1938. The eastern side of Oklahoma was the area from which most of the "Okies," many of them sharecroppers, migrated to California. But Tulsa still had a substantial oil industry and the nearby area, which included Hominy, did not suffer so much as the terrible Dust Bowl region on the western side.

So young Kenneth went off to the University of Oklahoma at Norman to start his higher education and pledged the Acacia Fraternity.

But neither Taylor nor Welch was enthralled by college life. There was too much going on in the world to sit around a campus in Norman, Oklahoma or West Lafayette, Indiana. So both joined the Army Air Corps to train as pilots, the former when he finished two and a half years at Purdue and the latter just as he would have been starting his junior year at Oklahoma.

Taylor after joining the Air Corps was sent to the Spartan College of Aeronautics and Technology in Tulsa, not far from his home in Hominy. From Spartan he was ordered to Randolph Field near San Antonio for basic training and then on to Brooks Field, also in the San Antonio area, for his advanced flight training earning the silver wings and gold bars of a second lieutenant.

These new Army officers who had not gone through the four years to graduate from West Point were known as "shave-tails."

This was because as officers they were required to have button-down epaulettes on the shoulders of their shirts. To salvage a regular Army shirt, the new officers would have tailors take the matching cloth needed for the epaulettes from material in the tails.

When both Taylor and Welch received their wings and commissions as second lieutenants, Welch a few months before Taylor, both were given their choices to be with a fighter squadron in Hawaii.

Both purchased cars after arriving on the island. But shortly after Welch's mother had left for the mainland and Delaware, a Honolulu cop had lifted his driver's license for making an illegal left turn and then, having had a little too much to drink, giving the officer some lip.

Thus the Taylor Buick had become their sole means of continuing a party routine on weekends which usually started on Waikiki Beach, moved on to the Officers' Club at Hickam Field near Pearl Harbor and ending up in the early morning hours at the Wheeler club next to their quarters.

That afternoon after flying around the island until their fuel was low, the two flights landed and the squadron aircraft turned over to the ground crews.

There was a cool trade winds breeze blowing in from the Pacific, which made living in the olive drab tents not unpleasant. After showers, the pilots put on their starched khakis and gathered in the makeshift, squad-tent Officers' Club for beer.

Both Taylor and Welch had enormous curiosities. So while Welch chatted with 2nd Lt. Lou Nagy, the squadron armament officer, Taylor noticed someone had brought that day's Honolulu Advertiser newspaper to the club and he scanned the front page.

It was difficult to ignore the major headlines. One read, "Japan Still Holds Hope of Peaceful Settlement." Others were more ominous warnings such as "Nippon Told to Sink U.S. Ships," "Blast Japan Off Seas" and still another said, "British Fleet Steams into Singapore."

As a newly commissioned second lieutenant Ken Taylor had no idea about what the combined military's strategy was should the country end up in a war with Japan. After graduation at Brooks, he couldn't recall any of his fellow pilots being too unhappy about being sent for duty in the Philippines, which would be one of the front lines in a war with the Japanese.

Japan already was spread thin with its conquests in China and French Indochina. It was hard to imagine it would be stupid enough to get into a war with the United States, but then few had envisioned what Hitler had done, also with a small country, in his military conquests in Europe.

Nagy had finished his beer and left to grab a stainless steel tray and get in the chow line. Welch, still working on his beer, looked over to scan the headlines on the Advertiser.

He laughed.

"Grits, you know those headlines remind me of a story."

"Go ahead and tell it," said Taylor, "as if I could stop you."

"Well," said Welch, "this first-grade teacher decides to start her class one morning by asking all the kids to stand up one at a time and give the class a 'happy thought.'

"So a little girl stands and says, 'We're going to the circus this weekend' and another kid says, 'My grandparents are coming to visit.'

"Next, this little girl stands up and says, 'I'm pregnant.'

"Most of the kids didn't even know what she meant, but the teacher was pretty surprised and asked the little girl, 'Honey, why would you say something like that?'

"The little girl stood up again and faced the teacher.

"When we were having breakfast this morning," she said, "my mom said she was pregnant and daddy said, 'That's a happy thought.'"

Taylor chuckled at the story but wasn't sure about the point George was making.

"The deal is everybody already has us on a ship going over to get in a war with Germany," Welch said. "But those headlines look like we might have our hands full out here in the Pacific. And ain't that a happy thought, fighting a war based on a vacation paradise island in Hawaii."

"I was just hoping that if we go to Europe some of those old RAF guys could give us some pointers on dealing with the German pilots," said Taylor. "But if we get into a war with the Japs, who the hell is going to clue us in on how to out fly their Zeroes?"

"You're asking me?" said George, "and all I think I know is the Zero supposedly has no armor protecting the pilot and nothing to protect its fuel tanks. But they are light and fast and I'm guessing most of their pilots by now have more combat hours than we have just soaring around over beautiful Hawaii."

Most of the officers had arisen to get into the chow line so Ken and George got up to join them.

"The P-40s are good airplanes," said Taylor. "The way the captain has pushed us, I can't say I'm really afraid to mix it up with the Zeroes. It don't matter whether we fight the Krauts or the Japs, our training will either pay off or we'll let the other guys get the best of us and end up splattered all over a cockpit, land in the middle of the English Channel or be eaten by sharks in the Pacific. Hell, I didn't join the Air Corps to peel spuds, so whatever happens we just take our chances."

"You're right," said Welch, picking up one of the bent up old trays. "I'm ready, just so I don't end up with a loser wing man like you."

Taylor already had his tray and was standing in front of Welch.

"If you can't fly any better than you can play cards," he said, "you better hope you'll be lucky enough to have a good old Okie covering your ass."

Current events of that day: *In Honolulu The Liberty House advertised evening skirts at $10.95. JAPAN GIVES TWO WEEKS MORE TO NEGOTIATIONS (headline). The British lost 19 bombers in raids on several German cities. An iron lung arrived in Hawaii for Queen's Hospital. On the New York stock exchange Woolworth gained two points up from 24 to 26 1/8. In Washington the House passed a bill permitting 15-round title boxing bouts in Hawaii and Alaska. At the Liberty Theatre in Honolulu, Abbott and Costello and Dick Powell were in the cast of the movie "In the Navy" with the Andrews Sisters.*

December 2, 1941

"As war clouds gathered over the Pacific and the intensity of alerts, exercises, and other training activities increased, Hawaii's military community as a whole still maintained a peacetime mentality and continued to operate with a business-as-usual attitude."
—"7 December 1941 The Air Force Story," p. 47

By Tuesday morning the red tape had been sorted out at Wheeler and the 47th was ready with aircraft armed with .30 caliber ammo and pilots eager to start pushing the buttons on their sticks sending real bullets through the flag target.

The ground crews had painted the front, bullet part of the rounds in different colors so the accuracy of each pilot's color could later be examined.

Capt. Austin and Lt. Rogers had decided that while the aircraft of one flight took turns firing at the flag target out over the water, the other flight would be practicing more aerial combat over the island in the general vicinity of Haleiwa.

The 47th squadron had been formed in December of 1940 by Capt. Austin when Taylor and Welch were still Air Corps flying cadets in training.

Austin started with no planes and no personnel. But as a West Pointer he knew something about how the Army system worked and soon had put together an organization that at least resembled a squadron.

After joining the 47th in January, 1941, it did not take long for Welch to impress Austin and Rogers with his extraordinary flying and aerial combat skills.

The same was true for Taylor when he arrived at the 47th in May fresh from advanced flight training at Brooks Field, San Antonio.

Austin was intrigued with both the young pilots. Their general flying abilities and fearlessness in practicing aerial combat offset the somewhat less than proper officer behavior on the ground. Their goofing off did not particularly bother him, but it drove Rogers with his own West Point background to endless frustration.

When the squadron was practicing aerial combat tactics with no nonsense, Austin particularly found Taylor and Welch adept at nailing their opponents and usually left Rogers trying to get into position to down Welch's P-40. Austin often chose Taylor as his aerial opponent and sometimes would have been the loser had it been real warfare.

Not that he didn't have some of the same attitude reflected by Taylor and Welch as a young officer just out of the Point. Austin felt the major challenge he and Rogers faced was keeping the squadron's pilots focused and not being so West Point rigid on the ground.

Many men new to the military chafed at the endless routines of marching, target practice with various weapons and keeping living quarters clean and orderly.

It was natural for newcomers to view these routines as somewhat of a way for senior officers to amuse themselves with their power. The longer they served the more they understood the routines were time-tested disciplinary measures keeping troops, whether on the ground or in the air, prepared to give their best in destroying an enemy with minimum harm to themselves.

On the second day at Haleiwa, Rogers was flying above the flag target practice while Austin cruised around at 10,000 feet watching the simulated aerial combat below him.

Two of the P-40s were chasing each other all over the sky. Disgusted, he got on his radio.

"Leader calling No. 161," Austin yelled. "Get into a split 'S' for God's sake before we have to send your parents a telegram that some Jap has nailed your ass."

The pilot in the sights of the P-40 on his tail took Austin's advice and moved into the maneuver he had been ordered to use, escaping to get into a position to be shooting at the other plane.

The truth was, in Austin's opinion, this squadron as a group was not ready for aerial combat anywhere, regardless of almost a year of intense training. Off the radio, he pushed the throttle of his own plane and moved the stick to the left, turning to watch different planes chasing each other.

Rogers, circling above the flag target practice just off the beach, was no happier about what was happening below him.

From the path of tracers used by the attacking P-40s it was easy to see some of the pilots were not even close to hitting the target but fortunately not endangering the old plane and its crew pulling the target. Shaking his head, he got on his radio.

"Gentlemen, the idea in this exercise is to hit the target. You are never going to do that until you learn to lead your target so you quit wasting your ammo way behind the flag. Lead your target, lead your target and I want to see some hits down there-- preferably on the flag!"

Late that afternoon in the headquarters tent, Austin and Rogers both were pacing around shaking their heads trying to diagnose the action of both flights that day and the apparent lack of readiness.

Austin was a pleasant man, older and wiser than his young charges in the 47th squadron and reluctant to beat up on them for their performances. Unlike Rogers, he believed leadership by example was better than using the club so often a part of military training not just for Americans but in military services all over the world.

Finally he looked over at the noncom sitting at the desk with the phone.

"Corporal, I want to talk to the pilots so get on the PA and tell all of them to get here on the double. Check the showers and latrines. I want *everybody* here on the double!"

Some fifteen minutes later Austin and Rogers counted heads of the pilots in front of the headquarters tent and decided all were present.

Both men pushed the tent flaps aside. Rogers called the squadron to attention, then ordered the pilots to be at ease.

They were a fine looking group of young men, Austin felt as he looked them over carefully, all dressed in their starched khakis.

In his heart he knew in a few weeks they would be in combat somewhere, somehow. Some would be exceptional pilots and, if lucky, live longer than the others who through either sloppy flying or bad luck would be dead or missing in action.

Whatever the circumstances, it would be his obligation to sit down and write a letter to the pilot's survivors, most likely parents, to console them in their loss. But he was the one with the captain's bars, soon to be the gold oak leaves of a major, on his uniform and that was just part of a squadron commander's job.

"Gentlemen, Lt. Rogers and I agree from watching the simulated aerial combat and shooting at the flag target that today was not our finest hour."

Several men, all smokers, cleared their throats not knowing what was coming next.

"Some of you have played sports and I'm sure everybody has at least watched a basketball or football game somewhere in high school or college.

"So let's take basketball as an example because it is more widely played than football since it takes fewer players. You have two teams under the basket at one end of the court and a player gets the ball and makes the fast break toward the other end of the court. In seconds, just mere seconds, he has made a lay-up and put two points on the board for his team.

"Or football," said the captain, who knew the game well. "You have a play by the offensive team, a fast back breaks through the line or a receiver catches a pass and within seconds those listening on the radio hear the announcer say, 'He's at the forty, the thirty, the twenty, the ten and now he's in the end zone for a touchdown,' and his team has six points.

"These things happen in just seconds.

"When we get into combat, as I'm sure we will in the next few weeks, I want you to remember that downing the other plane as opposed to you being shot down is mainly a matter of focus."

Taylor and Welch were standing together and exchanged a glance indicating they were wondering where Austin was going.

"What I'm talking about here," Austin continued, "is focus. F-o-c-u-s. Up there today, Lt. Rogers and I observed, it looked like you men were worrying about your dates Saturday night, your car payments, if your girl friend back home is playing around with some other guy or God knows how many thoughts other than about trying to be the best pilots in the Army Air Corps.

"So, what is my point? When we get into combat, you lose your focus for a few seconds it's not going to be a nice lay-up with your opponents scoring two points or a touchdown with six.

"In a few seconds in aerial combat, if you are not focused then your parents get a yellow Western Union telegram, I write a letter saying nice things about you, the Army gives you a white cross in some cemetery and life goes on.

"Just remember this. The odds are life will go on a lot longer for you if you stay focused every second in combat. Every second. And tomorrow, Lt. Rogers and I had better see some focus because we frankly like having you around. We're proud of the 47th squadron. We're proud of you. Let's get up in the morning feeling we are the best and then go out and demonstrate it."

Austin turned to leave then reversed himself and held up a hand to stop Rogers from dismissing the pilots.

"I also want to mention something going around out here that is more than just another rumor. The story is Gen. Short thinks we Air Corps people are just a bunch of flyboys up watching the scenery every day, and some of us should be out marching with the ground troops, digging latrines and trenches for water pipelines to those new tents at Wheeler and that kind of work.

"It's not at the level of my rank to try to convince him we are working hard at what we are supposed to be doing in the Army, and that is flying planes that can do a lot of damage to any enemy. Let's not give him any reason to be inspired to expand on what he already has started which I personally think is a grave error. Whether or not Gen. Martin, commander of the Hawaiian Air Force or Gen. Davidson, the 14th Pursuit Wing commander, can convince him otherwise I don't know. But I damn sure hope they will be falling on the sword trying to keep us doing what the Army Air Force is supposed to do."

With that, Austin turned and went back into the headquarters tent while Rogers dismissed the men so they could head for the evening meal.

Taylor and Welch walked away together. Regardless of their cocky bravado appearance, both had their doubts about what would happen when up in the sky against veteran enemy pilots trying to shoot them down.

"Woo," mused Welch. "Somebody got up on the wrong side of the bed this morning."

"George, for Christ's said," said Taylor, mild anger in his voice. "The captain isn't out here just to give us a lot of crap. You know how sloppy some of those guys were today. Shit, they looked like little bear cubs playing with their dicks."

"Okay, okay," said George. "I know he's right. But I bet your old man just like mine told you a hundred times to stop doing something that would be a screwup and you didn't listen.

"With some of these pilots, they are not going to get the idea until we are in combat and they see one of our P-40s heading for the ground with smoke and flames coming out and it will be, 'Aloha, old buddy.'"

After the evening meal as some of the pilots were sitting in the club drinking beer, Taylor in his sly, casual way suggested maybe they could play a little poker.

Most 47th squadron pilots knew of Taylor's skill at the card game. But, at the same time the daring-do egos that led them into the Army Air Corps and through the tough training to get their wings also made most feel they should not be intimidated by the guy from Oklahoma, especially those from California who considered Okies to be no more than a rag-tag lot even if they had been to college.

A pilot produced a new deck of cards, the version of the game was decided on and cards dealt.

One Californian was especially disdainful of Taylor to his back. With his buddies he made jokes about Ken being a "cotton picker" with his relatives heading west with a mattress on the roof of an old car and six ragamuffin kids hanging out the window.

So it was he and two of his buddies who had been at Stanford before they joined the Air Corps sat down for the game. Welch, nursing a beer, had decided to let Taylor do the playing. If he won some money, maybe for once he would pick up a check or two if they were not on duty and out partying come the weekend.

In the first half hour Taylor had losing hands and Welch was beginning to worry he would end up losing everything he had won on Saturday night at the Wheeler club.

Emboldened by Taylor's misfortunes, the Californians ordered more beer and began to up the ante. With every hand, the Oklahoman painfully reached into his pocket and slowly peeled off the bills he needed to stay in the game.

"Hey," said one of the pilots. "Let's sing *our* school song and let the Okie hear something from a real school!"

His two companions, who also were amassing a little money in front of them, yelled "Yea, let's sing him a *good* school song."

So the three joined in loudly, reflecting the influence of their beer.

"Oh, it's beer, beer, beer that gives us all a cheer on the farm, on the farm.

"It's beer, beer, beer that gives us all a cheer on the Leland Stanford Junior Farm!"

No emotion appeared on Taylor's face as he studied the cards that had just been dealt to him before the singing began.

"Oh, it's wine, wine, wine that makes us feel so fine on the farm, on the farm.

"Yes it's wine, wine, wine that makes us feel so fine on the Leland Stanford Junior Farm."

The singers paused a minute to take big swigs from the beer bottles and play a few cards. Then the leader started up again.

"Oh, it's whiskey..."

"What do you say we hold that a minute," said Taylor softly. "It's getting late, so why don't we just all bet that famous farm on the next hand."

"You got it, Okie," said one of the Californians. And all four players shoved their money into a pile in the center of the table. One dealt the cards requested by the other players, took another swig of beer, and was ready for the next verse of their song with each pausing long enough to pass or draw more cards.

"Oh, it's whiskey, whiskey, whiskey that makes us all so frisky on the farm, on the farm.

"Yes it's whiskey, whiskey, whiskey that makes us all so frisky on the Leland Stanford Junior Farm."

The hand had played out and it was time now to show cards. One by one the Californians laid them down, completely assured they had nailed the hayseed Okie.

The others had good cards but they were yet to see what Taylor was holding. Slowly, as he looked at each man at the table he laid down a card. An ace of diamonds,

JOHN MARTIN MEEK

an ace of clubs and an ace of hearts. He hesitated for a moment then placed the final card on the table. It was the ace of spades.

The Californians could not believe it but there were the cards on the table and Taylor raked in the pot, carefully pocketing the money.

"Nice to play with you boys," he said, getting up from his chair. "And I especially enjoyed that song about your farm. What do they grow on it besides poor crops of card players?"

The three Stanford alums stomped out of the tent. Welch waited until they were out of earshot and literally bent over double laughing, slapping Taylor hard on the back.

"Man, that was the funniest thing I've seen since I've been in Hawaii."

"Well, George," drawled Taylor, "we have a saying back in Oklahoma. When our morons go out to California, it raises the IQ level of both states."

Current events of that day: United Press reported 75,000 Japanese troops in position to strike at Thailand. Americans left Shanghai on "Last Chance" vessel. Soviet Tanks Repulse Nazis at Moscow. U.S. House of Representatives passed drastic restrictions on defense industry strikes. Judge Brooks granted 17 divorce decrees in Honolulu. Maxim Litvinov, new Soviet ambassador to the U.S. would be arriving Thursday from Singapore on the China Clipper. Edith Peters, 8, of Mission Lane in Kakaako personally delivered her letter to Santa to him in the lobby of the Honolulu Advertiser. The Philippines Declared in Great Peril (headline).

December 3, 1941

"The intense training took its toll in flying mishaps that resulted in a number of deaths and serious injuries, but it was the younger, inexperienced pilots who usually made up the accident statistics."
—"7 December 1941 The Air Force Story," p. 44.

Wednesday morning as Capt. Austin and Lt. Rogers cruised above the 47th's aerial combat and flag target practice it was obvious the squadron commander's straightforward talk the previous evening had made an impact on all the pilots. Viewing the action as the two leaders' P-40s cruised at 7,000 feet over the Haleiwa area there was a day-night difference between what was then happening and the practice on Tuesday.

After an hour in "another Hawaii day in paradise" morning, Austin called to Rogers on the radio.

"Bob, I think it's time we get down there and mix it up with the boys. We can always use some spring training ourselves."

"What did you have in mind, sir?"

"I'll take on Welch first while you get in line with those shooting at the flag. Then, before we land for lunch we can swap so you can see how Taylor is doing today."

"Sounds good," said Rogers. Communicating the plan on the radio to Lt. Taylor whose flight was leading the flag practice, he put the P-40 into a big, sweeping arc to reach the altitude of the old B-10 bomber aircraft pulling the target.

Austin radioed Welch then began maneuvering his P-40 to get into position for starting the simulated combat with his other flight leader.

Having begun his career in a peacetime Army, Austin had no combat experience but he did have one advantage. When he was in flight school some of the instructors still were aerial combat veterans of World War I.

While his P-40 was vastly superior to the old biplane Spads and others used in World War I, still in combat there was a limited number of maneuvers a pilot could make regardless of the aircraft he was flying.

The PT-17 Stearman biplane that was the standard for Army Air Corps flight training could turn on a dime whereas the P-40 at its top speed around 350 MPH needed a lot of space for a turn, as it did for the Japanese Zero and the German's Messerschmitt fighter.

But now the World War I fighter pilots had mostly climbed in rank and no longer were flight instructors, so the newer pilots such as Taylor and Welch had not been beneficiaries of their experience in the air over France and Germany.

Still, as far as Austin was concerned aerial combat basically was a chess game with the player who was smartest and not afraid of taking chances usually coming out the victor.

The tactic used by the 47th Squadron to start aerial combat practice was for both fighters to put some distance between each other, but still be within eyesight. Then, each plane would turn to face and fly toward the other. As they passed in a little game of "chicken," the aerial combat practice would begin.

As Welch peeled off from the game he was playing with another 47th pilot and made the "chicken" pass with Austin's P-40, his leader positioned himself to the east so Welch would have to seek him out facing the sun.

Many pilots liked the P-40, feeling it to be a fine aircraft. For others the plane came down to what indeed it was, a modified version of the older P-36 which some pilots were still flying in Hawaii waiting for more of the newer P-40s to arrive.

The P-40s had the 1,040 horsepower Allison V-1710 supercharged, 12-cylinder V engine. It's maximum speed was well over 350 miles an hour with a ceiling of almost 33,000 feet.

While less maneuverable in the sky than the Japanese Zero or German Messerschmitt fighters, the P-40 provided much more protection for its pilots with armor plating around the cockpit and self-sealing fuel tanks.

For armament the P-40B had two .50 caliber guns atop the engine and two .30 caliber guns firing from both wings, which made it quite lethal when an enemy plane came into the gunsights mounted in front and slightly to the right of the pilot's wind screen.

Another of the P-40's major pluses was in dives, so Austin carefully maneuvered his aircraft into position to swoop down on Welch while being careful to keep between the sun and his "enemy."

Welch had closed his canopy, moved his goggles up on his helmet and donned aviator-style sunglasses. And not far in the distance he saw his squadron leader in the dive putting him on the edge of the P-40's maximum speed.

It was his instant guess that Austin was going below him to pull out of the dive and be in the position of cranking off rounds into his P-40's belly—a vulnerable part of the aircraft.

The young pilot had guessed right, and put his plane into a roll that left Austin passing harmlessly behind him

But Welch was not playing a game with an amateur. His leader immediately added full power and started climbing in a maneuver for an inside loop that again would give him the height for another chance at a kill.

Welch looking back saw what he figured would be the captain's next move and the question with only seconds to come up with an answer was, "What the hell do I do now?"

Quickly he eased back the throttle and simultaneously pulled back on the stick, and his bird with no power and the nose up went into a stall followed by a steep, spiraling dive. The verdant green on the terrain below was coming up fast until he gave the plane full throttle and pulled out a few hundred feet above the ground.

Once again Capt. Austin's strategy to finish off one of his flight leaders had failed. Instead of being annoyed at the clever flying of his young charge, the squadron commander was proud he had an opponent providing a real challenge.

Ever since Welch had joined the squadron in January new out of flight school, Austin had been trying to find weaknesses in the young lieutenant's flying skills.

Almost a year later he still had not found much.

Over that year Welch's boundless energy needing to be in the air, studying his P-40 on the ground or being ready for a party any time any place had earned him the nickname of "Wheaties," the popular cereal known by Americans as "The Breakfast of Champions."

When Taylor joined the squadron in May and developed a close friendship with Welch, his friend learned he came from a town in Oklahoma called Hominy and thus the nickname of "Grits" came into being.

The riding he took from the Californians for being an "Okie" or from Welch and other 47th pilots who took up the "Grits" nickname did not faze him.

"Taylor," Welch said one morning over breakfast chow, "if I'm going to be Wheaties, then you are going to be Grits. Funny because breakfast is not exactly our favorite meal, especially when we can sleep in."

Austin now had 25 planes in his 47th squadron and the actual flying time was by no means unlimited.

The pilots spent hours studying weather patterns which they would definitely have to deal with wherever they flew.

Sitting on their butts in the hangars or in the shade of the planes, Austin and Rogers had training sessions where the mechanics talked to them about what might go wrong with the Allison engines on takeoff, landings and in the air. It was a great engine but not one without fault as Taylor was the first in the 47th to learn one day.

His flight path had taken "Grits" high and out over the Pacific when suddenly he was looking at a propeller in front of him that was not turning and the smooth roar of the Allison was no more. His powerful P-40 had become a glider.

"Operations," Taylor called on his radio, "this is 155 and it, uh, looks like I've got myself an engine failure up here."

There was a long pause before a response came from operations. After all, this was not a situation it dealt with every day.

"Uh, 155, can you give us your position?"

"I was at 10,000 when the engine died," came Taylor's calm reply. "Estimate I'm, oh, about five miles from Haleiwa."

"Have you gone though all the routine procedures for restarting the engine?" asked the voice on the radio from operations, generally referred to as "ops."

"Roger," drawled Taylor. "She ain't gonna start for me and I'm not much more than a rock with wings on it at the present time. Down to 8,000 and falling pretty fast."

Again a long pause from ops.

"Aircraft 155, we have done some quick calculations down here and you can't make it back. Check your life jacket and prepare to abandon your ship immediately," came the reluctant order from ops. The P-40s were not a dime a dozen in Hawaii and the brass hated to lose one.

In the cockpit Taylor also had done some quick calculations, some from training and some from just plain seat of the pants flying. This time the long pause was from him as he listened to the wind going over the wings and by the cockpit with the canopy closed to reduce drag.

"Ops," he said, "you guys are ordering me to bail out over the most shark-infested waters around the island. That makes no sense to me. At least I need to get back over land."

"Uh, 155, we have done the calculations and you are not going to make it back over land at your altitude and glide speed. Lieutenant, you are ordered to bail out immediately. I repeat, go though the correct procedures. We have more aircraft but we don't have more pilots. And we're calling the pick up boats at Haleiwa and the Navy right now to get a PBY in the air to pick you up from your estimated point of contact with the water."

"Wait a minute, wait a cotton pickin' minute, ops," Taylor lied. "The prop is starting to turn a little so maybe she's going to start up again."

Off in the distance far beyond the shiny, deep blue water and white caps on the waves he could see the field. Going in dead stick was no problem because of the relatively short distance the P-40 would roll before it stopped. He knew because he had once cut his engine before landing to test the dead-stick technique.

"Aircraft 155," came the radio voice from ops, "if the engine was going to start it would have by now. Bail out of your aircraft and that is an order!"

A decision now had to be made in seconds. Sure, the lumbering old Navy PBY probably wouldn't have too much trouble spotting him in the water.

But only two weeks previously a surfer had lost a leg to a shark in that area. Moreover, his chute might get entangled and drag him under, and just wearing his yellow Mae West life jacket he would not be a cinch to be spotted in the ocean by the Navy boys. Then there was the problem of whether the PBY could land because from up there he could not judge the height of the waves.

Taylor had a large number of options going through his mind. He thought momentarily about obeying the order but that passed in an instant. He would rather face a court martial than the big jaws of a shark.

"Uh, ops, Taylor here. I can see the field now so I'm going to ride 'er down. Appreciate your help but I think I can make it."

"Aircraft 155," the voice on the radio from operations yelled furtively, "bail out of your aircraft. We don't give a damn where you are, do not ride it down. We need you, Taylor, for Christ's sake get out of that plane!"

Getting into a panic mode was not in Ken Taylor's genes. That was why he had been chosen almost directly out of flight school to be a flight leader in the 47th Squadron, why he always seemed to do well at the poker table and maintained a cool attitude wherever he happened to be.

Gliding down he had opened his canopy slightly and without the roaring noise of the Allison engine only the wind passing by was a sound in his ears.

Now he knew he had beat the odds, that the P-40 was going to hit the smooth steel of the PSP with the light brown sand oozing up through the mesh forming the runway.

The P-40's wheels hit down just as the runway began near the beach, and he needed not apply the brakes too much to bring the ship to a stop up near the tents just short of where a few other squadron P-40s were on the ramp.

The field's fire engine with siren blasting followed him down the runway and at the docks in Haleiwa Army rescue boats had been out circling offshore standing by. Ground crew and pilots came rushing out to greet Taylor as he snapped off his seat harness, pulled the canopy all the way back and stood to get out of the cockpit.

A pilot named McKeon was the first to reach the plane.

"Taylor, you sonofabitch, you did it but ops is going to have your ass for not bailing out when the engine quit."

Taylor was on the wing and stepped down onto the ramp, shedding his Mae West life jacket and tossing it back into the cockpit.

"Somebody's going to get it sooner or later I reckon," said Taylor, referring to his butt. "It may be a Kraut or Jap or shark but the least of my worries is some desk jockey over at ops.

"They said we got lots of planes and not enough pilots. That's just bullshit. If we got lots of planes, then why are some of our Wheeler pilots flying P-36s and other old planes? So in this case they got their pilot *and* the plane back."

McKeon, who hardly knew Taylor, laughed and the two pilots walked away to where they could stop and light cigarettes.

"Nice going, Taylor," said McKeon, slapping his fellow pilot on the back. "Nice going."

The next person to greet Taylor was the corporal from the squadron command office.

He was a small, slender Italian man with a wisp of a mustache and beak nose that always seemed to be sniffing something.

The corporal saluted.

"Sir, Capt. Austin would like to see you on the double!"

Taylor returned the salute, nodded and swiftly walked towards the squadron tent. Waiting inside was the captain signing papers and looking over other documents relating to the maintenance of the unit's aircraft.

Coming to attention in front of Austin's desk, Taylor saluted but said nothing.

Austin looked up, nodded and told his young flight leader to sit. Sighing, the squadron leader leaned back in his chair.

"Wheeler called me and you have a big problem over at ops," he said. "You disobeyed a direct order by not bailing out after your engine quit."

"Sir," said Taylor, lighting another Lucky. "I was up there. I was the one who was going to have to bail out in the ocean. I was the commander of my ship, the one who knew the most about what it could and could not do. I figured it could make it back. Sitting over in the middle of the island, what the hell did ops know?"

"It's not *what* they know, lieutenant, it is they know who they are and the power they have. You in effect told them to go screw themselves, and that does not go over well in this man's army."

"Captain, if they want to court martial me so be it. But you know as well as I do that we don't have a surplus of P-40s. If we get shipped out to the Philippines or some place like that one plane could make a helluva lot of difference.

"Sir, I admit I was thinking about my own ass. But I also was considering the future and how scarce the new P-40s are out here."

"Look, Ken, I understand. Back at the Point we had an old instructor who flew with Eddie Rickenbacker in World War I. He told us one day, 'Gentlemen, the biggest risk you have to take in combat is disobeying an order when you feel *you* know what is best to do.'

"You and Welch are risk takers. That's why Lt. Rogers and I made you flight leaders. And nobody but a fool would understand that any day we're going to be in a war. And in a war we are going to need risk takers.

"I'll talk to Col. Flood and Gen. Davidson and explain the situation. In short, I'm going to try to save you from a *big* dressing down. But, just remember this, Taylor. If I can convince the brass you did the right thing even against orders, you owe me. You really owe me."

Taylor stood and saluted.

"Sir, thank you. But we got to find out what made that engine quit out there. The way I see it, bailing out over water is nothing compared to having a dead stick with a Kraut or Jap on my tail. Now that would be a problem."

"I'll talk to the crew chiefs," said Austin. "Dismissed."

Back in the sky earlier that day, in the aerial combat duel between Austin and Welch, a cat and mouse game had continued as each skillfully managed to avoid giving the other a decent shot at his plane.

As Austin had ordered on the first day at Haleiwa, Welch had begun anew to study the island and its topography. He knew that by getting low enough the dull, olive drab color of his plane would provide some camouflage flying in the shallow canyons between the island's hills. And that was where he went.

83

It was a dangerous gamble, not untypical of Welch's flying. If his squadron leader decided to use the same strategy, they might well collide where there would be no chance for either to survive.

Shortly Welch pushed the throttle all the way in and pulled back on the stick to execute a chandelle, a maneuver that would quickly gain altitude. At the top of his loop, he would right the plane and hope his quarry might be in its gunsights.

And sure enough there was Austin in his cockpit right in front of him looking in every direction for his quarry.

"Sir," came Welch's voice over the radio to Austin, "I have you in my sights. Sorry, sir, but this one's over."

"Sorry, hell, lieutenant, that's the kind of flying I've been trying to teach this squadron for the last year. Congratulations. Now let's go down and get some chow."

Current events of that day: *In Chicago, Marshall Field launched a new morning newspaper called the Sun. Japan accused Aussies of being "Japanophobes." The Honolulu Advertiser pled for help in providing a Merry Xmas (sic) for 3,200 needy children. Plans were for the "A Yank in the RAF" film to open at the Waikiki Theater on Friday night. Columnist Walter Winchell reported A. Jolson took an $800,000 loss in Wall Street. Endicott Peabody was named to the United Press All-America team, the last football player at Harvard earning that honor. A six-pack of Coca-Cola sold for 25 cents at Walter's Market in Honolulu.*

December 4, 1941

Early in the week Taylor hitched a ride on an Army supply truck to Wheeler to bring his Buick back to Haleiwa so he and Welch had transportation.

Thursday afternoon after gunnery practice they cleaned up, changed from flight suits to the obligatory starched khakis, chowed down and drove to the Wheeler club.

Sitting at the bar they ordered beers but were shortly interrupted when another second lieutenant approached them looking for someone to join in a poker game.

He introduced himself as Hans Christiansen of the 44th Pursuit Squadron.

Taylor did not hesitate to accept.

"We're with the 47th and just came over from gunnery practice at Haleiwa," Taylor said, "but my buddy here has never needed any help drinking so count me in."

After Ken left George sat staring ahead at the mirrored back of the bar seeing himself as he sipped his Bud.

The week at Haleiwa had been the best since he joined the 47th in January, being thrilled every time he pushed the red button on his P-40's stick and heard the rare sound of his machine guns as he made passes at the flag target.

He felt good about besting his squadron commander in the mock dogfight. Still, he could not help wonder what it would be like in the air against a German or a Jap pilot most likely in any situation one with combat experience.

The story was the Japanese didn't have good eyesight. Though he was too cynical to believe tales such as that going around, it obviously would be an edge in any aerial combat situation.

Every military person in Hawaii who didn't have their heads up their butts must know the country would be in a war in the next few weeks.

Army pilots were not so many they were falling all over each other wherever they were based, back in the States or elsewhere. When the bell rang, he and the other pilots in Hawaii would be headed for the action as quick as they could get there.

Welch knew he was a good pilot with lots of skill from his year training with Capt. Austin, Lt. Rogers and the 47th. What he did not know was how much courage there might be within himself the first time facing an enemy. However it went, he hoped he would make his parents back in Wilmington proud and earn the respect of the some 200 men in the squadron.

Then something caught his eye and still looking at the bar mirror he saw a petit, attractive redhead sit down on the last stool to his left.

There were many single women on the island either civilians or those few in the military who might be guests at the officers' clubs. He knew Fort Shafter had a large hospital but its nurses seldom had been seen socializing at Wheeler.

The young woman was dressed in a summery, flowered frock with her hair in the fashion of the famous Andrews Sisters trio.

Always relaxed and confident with women, George picked up his beer and walked over to the end of the bar.

"I'm George Welch," he said as she turned to face him. "If you're not with someone else I'd like to join you."

There was a slight hesitation as the bartender set a drink on the bar in front of the woman, something that looked like a Coke.

"I'm Flo," she responded with a slight smile as she looked at George.

"Flo? That's it?" said George, putting his beer on the bar and sitting sideways on the barstool.

Flo took a sip from her glass and then looked at the bar mirror, her chin up in the air, slightly disdainful.

"I don't mind telling people my whole name. I just get tired of them laughing when I do."

"Aw, c'mon," said George with his lopsided smile. I promise I will not laugh at your name. Okay?"

"It's Florence Nightingale."

George as promised didn't laugh.

"And," he said, "of course you're a nurse."

"That's right," said Flo. "Guess it runs in the family."

"Don't tell me you're actually related to the real Florence Nightingale."

"Yep, buster," said Flo. "My grandparents are from England and I'm supposed to be a great, great, grand niece or something like that."

"Notice I didn't laugh?"

"Noticed you wanted to."

"You here at Wheeler? I guess we have nurses here but so far I haven't needed one. Uh, let me correct that. So far I haven't been sick."

"George," said Flo, "your pickup line isn't exactly sick but it could use some treatment. No, I'm not at Wheeler. I'm a surgical nurse at Tripler Hospital at Fort Shafter."

George laughed. Flo was a little sassy and he liked that.

"Hey," he said, "somebody just put some money in the jukebox. Wanna dance?"

Flo said nothing but arose and started walking toward the club's dance floor.

George had learned and liked to dance while a student at Purdue. He found in Flo a partner who was as talented and smooth as any coed he had ever known during his university years.

They danced to three songs.

The second was "Fools Rush In," and from the beginning notes Flo moved closer to George as he tightened his arms around her, and they danced alone on the floor with a few dozen envious single officers interrupting their drinking and talk to admire the young pilot's apparent good luck.

The next song coming up on the juke box was "Chattanooga Choo Choo," and the dancers switched into a frantic but well executed jitterbug that left them a little breathless as they walked back to the bar holding hands.

After they were seated again, Flo took a drink then turned to her companion.

"I see you're a pilot. What are you doing here at Wheeler?"

"I'm with the 47th, a fighter squadron. Right now we're at gunnery practice at a little field on the North Shore called Haleiwa."

Flo stirred her drink with the straw in it.

"You guys are crazy. I hear some pilot wore a parachute under his tux at the Royal Hawaiian ballroom last Saturday night, and then pulled that thingofamajig that lets it go and the ceiling fans blew the silk all over the place."

"Kinda dumb, huh?"

"A nurse from Tripler who was there said it was really silly, but I thought it was funny. Wish I could have been there."

"That was me."

Flo whirled to look at George, eyes wide and mouth open in disbelief.

"That was you? You did that?"

"Yep," George said, with obvious pride. "This island life is laid back. We're just out here by ourselves. Why not have a little fun."

Flo leaned over and put an arm around him, laughing.

Both were quiet for a moment.

"George, do you think we're going to war?"

"We're going to war for sure, probably in the next few weeks."

"You mean with Germany? If we do I hope I get sent to England. I've never been there and I'm dying to see it."

A shrug.

"Who knows? I guess my preference would be to go to England where at least I could understand the language. But our squadron leader is convinced it will be with the Japs and we'll be sent to the Philippines."

Flo reached a hand over and put it on George's arm.

"I hope we both get sent to England. Wouldn't that be nice where everything is so old and lovely and green!"

She picked up her glass and drank deeply. Just in the short time they had been together at the club she obviously had become relaxed around George and comfortable in his presence.

"Say, uh, Flo. I rode over from Haleiwa with a buddy who's in that poker game. Excuse me while I go over and see how he's doing."

Flo squeezed his arm and smiled her answer.

Near the poker table Welch pulled up a chair next to Taylor, who was dealing the cards.

"You to the point you'll have to hock your watch yet?"

"Oh, win some, lose some," said Taylor.

Welch lowered his voice.

"Look, I met the gal over there at the bar..."

"So I noticed," Taylor interrupted.

"She's a nurse at Tripler and I'm going to ask her to go with me to my room. Okay if we stay over and go back to Haleiwa early tomorrow?"

"You know, Wheaties, for a guy who likes to fly as much as you do it just seems you are begging to get kicked out of the Army and sent home. It's against the regulations to have a gal in our room."

"Grits, how long do you think this little stay in paradise is going to last? A month from now we may both be dead or in our planes at the bottom of the Philippine Sea. Screw it. If she will go, I'm doing it."

George pushed back his chair and headed to the bar where he gave Flo a hug before he sat down on his stool.

About ten minutes later Taylor saw Welch and the nurse leaving the club, holding hands.

The Bachelor Officers' Quarters rooms were ample but sparse with a narrow steel bed, desk, two chairs, a chest of drawers and a rack for hanging up clothes. Midway in the building was the room with the toilets, showers and mirrors for shaving.

The two of them tiptoed down the hall and slipped into the room, where George immediately turned on a little radio tuned to some Hawaiian music.

"Oh, God," whispered Flo. "I've got to pee and I didn't think to do it before we left the club."

"You can't go down to the toilet," said George, also in a whisper. "Somebody may see you."

He looked around the room for a moment then spotted his old World War I "wash basin" helmet on a shelf.

"See that helmet?"

Flo nodded.

"Use it. I'm going to turn out the light and get in bed. But we got to be careful because I don't have a rubber."

There were giggles from the nurse and laughter from George in the darkness as sound of liquid hitting the steel filled the room. Then he felt a small warm body with the odor of lilac perfume slide under the sheet and blanket to lie close to him.

"We're both crazy, you know that?" she said.

In the darkness Flo could not see George's lopsided smile of pleasure and those were the last words spoken as he pulled her to him. As he bent to kiss her, from his subconscious came back the words from "Fools Rush In."

"Though I see

"The danger there

"If there's a chance for me

"Then I don't care."

Later lying in each other's arms, he broke the silence but with his voice low.

"I'm surprised you came over here with me."

"Why? Just because guys have dicks why are they the only ones who are supposed to enjoy sex?"

"You got me there."

"I do have you," whispered Flo. "So why don't you just shut up and make love to me again."

Current events of that day: *Probe of Japanese Activities Here (Honolulu) Will Be Made by Senate, Spy Inquiry Reportedly Gets Tentative O.K. By State Dept. COMPLETE COLLAPSE OF US-JAPAN TALKS LOOM. ROMMEL AT HEAD OF NAZI ATTACK (Honolulu Advertiser* *headlines). The House in Washington, DC debated the defense appropriations bill, increasing the Army to 2,000,000 men. Undefeated and untied Duquesne was being considered to play in the Sun Bowl in El Paso.*

December 5, 1941

"We learned Friday afternoon we would have the weekend off. They brought in the crews of the antiaircraft guns at Wheeler and everybody else not on duty turned in their weapons and ammo. Me and two buddies had a deal where the last one awake Saturday morning had to buy the steaks Saturday night in Honolulu."

—Former Sgt. Raymond Turley, 47th Squadron crew chief, in a telephone interview in the fall of 2007.

At about 4 p.m. on Friday, all the 47th P-40s were on the ground. The armament specialists had orders to take the ammo from the planes and lock it up. Ground crews parked the aircraft, but the plan was that they would not be refueled until the squadron began its second week of gunnery practice—mostly strafing targets at Bellows Field. Each plane was assigned a guard to protect it against sabotage from the Japanese locals under the Alert One orders for sabotage.

Sgt. Raymond Turley, a good old boy from Mt. Sterling, Kentucky, was finishing up what needed to be done to the plane Capt. Austin had been flying all week. After he closed the canopy and jumped off the wing onto the ground, he stuffed a greasy rag in a pocket of his gray/green ground crew overalls and walked over to where a friend was just finishing up with another P-40.

"Well, old buddy," he said in the Kentucky, slow-talking accent, "it's quitting time and no word yet from the captain about getting off or staying on duty this weekend."

"Makes no difference to me," said the friend, a corporal from New York, "I'm broke so I would just as soon stay here and go over on the beach awhile the next couple of days. "How about you?

"Reckon if we aren't on duty I wouldn't mind going down to Honolulu. Looking at some of those cute tourist gals on Waikiki Beach beats what I been seeing here all week."

"You bet," said the corporal, "we get a free weekend, maybe I can borrow a few bucks 'til payday and go with you."

In the headquarters tent, Capt. Austin was hanging up the phone when Lt. Rogers pushed back the heavy, waterproofed tent flap and walked in.

Austin turned to him.

"I was just talking to Wheeler about what's on the boards for this weekend." he said. "The word is the Navy is giving its men shore leave and Wheeler and the other bases same as here–Alert One for sabotage."

Rogers looked surprised. "You think that's smart with the way things are going with the Japs?"

He walked over to the sergeant's desk. Picking up that day's copy of the Honolulu Advertiser, he held the front page up for Austin to see.

"Pacific Zero Hour Near: Japan Answers US Today," a big headline read.

"We have no idea how many spies the Japs have on this island," said the squadron's operations officer, "or how they are armed or what kind of explosives they may have stuck away somewhere."

"A good point," said Austin. "But all the bases including this one have men on guard with small arms. What the hell kind of Army is this anyway if we can't take on a few Jap civilians if they try to make a move?"

"So, you have any plans for this weekend?"

"A few of us have been talking about taking a bomber over to Molokai to do a little deer hunting and check out some possible emergency landing sites," replied Austin. "That's not quite the same as hunting in Colorado or Wyoming, so I don't have strong feelings about the trip one way or the other. But some of the men really want to do it."

Rogers lit a cigarette and paced around the tent while Austin sat at his desk and propped his feet on top of it.

Rogers smiled.

"I don't remember what exactly at the Point prepared me for this stupid situation. What would we do if we keep the men on duty out here? With Gen. Short ordering all the planes lined up together in the middle of the field at Wheeler, as you've told me, if there were saboteurs we couldn't shoot at them without hitting our own aircraft. And if anything happened at night, we would be totally useless except for what we could do with small arms. Probably just end up shooting each other."

'It's our decision," said Austin. "Why don't you just flip a coin. Heads we're off for the weekend, tails we stay here on duty."

Rogers laughed, reaching into his pocket. "This may be a first in Army decision making."

He brought out a shiny quarter, flipped it into the air and watched the coin land on the floor.

"Sir, it's heads," said the non-com on duty at the desk.

"Okay," said Austin, rising. "Corporal, call Wheeler for trucks to come out and pick up the men who aren't doing duty, then get on the PA system and give them the word. Those who are leaving Haleiwa are to be back here by 0600 hours Monday."

"Yes sir!" said the non-com and grabbed the PA microphone.

Taylor and Welch were in their tents along with other pilots, most stripped down to shorts and undershirts waiting word on whether it was duty or no duty for the weekend, when the announcement came over the PA.

Taylor lit a cigarette and walked barefooted over to the tent where Welch was quartered.

"You know, George," said Taylor, taking a deep drag on his Lucky, "the longer I'm with the 47th the more I'm impressed with the captain's decisions."

"Damn tooting," said Welch. "What the hell would we do if some Jap saboteurs tried something with our planes out here? Hell, except for those on guard we're not even armed with anything unless we got a pocket knife."

"I think the top brass knows a bunch of us are going to be heading for England or the Philippines any day," responded Taylor. "So maybe they kind of view giving us this weekend off as a military version of the Last Supper."

Welch was sitting on the standard old olive drab canvas folding cot.

"I don't like these old cots one damned bit and there's nothing to do out here on the North Shore but go over to that old bar in Haleiwa for a few beers," he said. "You got your car here, why don't we head back to Wheeler and have some drinks and dinner at the club?"

"I never realized how easy it is to get people to make decisions for you until I joined the Army," said Taylor, "it's amazing, absolutely amazing."

"What's amazing to me about this man's army," said Welch, pulling on his khakis, "is that we found some organization that is dumb enough to pay us for being in paradise flying fighters and having the time of our lives."

A half hour later Taylor and Welch were dressed, had their bags packed and headed down the old macadam road for the ten-mile drive to Wheeler.

"So, Grits, what do you think we ought to do tomorrow night?" asked Welch. The windows of the Buick were open and the cool, salt air mixed freely with the smoke from the cigarettes both men were holding.

"Why not start down at the Royal Hawaiian?" Taylor responded. "Even if we don't see any available gals, it's a great place to drink, listen to music and watch the hula dancers."

"Suits me," said Welch. "Since we'll probably be stopping in at the Hickam and Wheeler clubs, remind me tomorrow to get my tux out of the cleaners. Otherwise they won't let me in under their elite 'you gotta wear a tux' rule."

After dinner at the club, the two young pilots chatted with other members of the 47th and pilots they knew only casually from other units on the base.

"So, George," asked Taylor, "how do you feel about our first week out at Haleiwa?"

"Damned good," said Welch. "And, boy, did I have some fun before I landed this afternoon."

"I'm afraid to ask what it was," sighed Taylor.

"There was some little place out there with a few houses so I was clipping along at about five hundred feet and I spotted this young girl hanging her panties out on a clothes line. I made a turn and came back over her about two hundred feet and the prop wash blew those panties all over her yard. She fell down on the lawn and when I looked back her dress had blown up and she wasn't wearing any pants. But she got to her feet shaking her fist at me. Boy, I loved it."

Taylor chuckled and looked in wonder at his buddy, who didn't seem to care what chances he took by putting his career in jeopardy. But he saw no reason to point out what might happen if the girl got his plane number and reported the buzzing incident to the Army high command.

"Sounds like you're kinda jumping the gun on our strafing practice at Bellows next week. Tell me, at what point in your life did you get into this mode of doing stupid stuff like scaring that poor little gal half to death?"

"I dunno," said Welch. "Pretty early on I guess. It just always seemed to me life has room for a few laughs as long as nobody gets hurt."

"That parachute stunt at the Royal Hawaiian must have topped them all."

"Nope," said Welch. "I think my best was when I was at St. Andrews, where I went to high school in Middletown, Delaware."

"Wait a minute, you're from Wilmington and you went to school in some other town?"

"It's what you call a prep school," said Welch. "I was there five years. My older brother, Dehn, went there, too. Kind of fun going off to school and being away from your parents for nine months of the year."

"Well," said Taylor, sarcastically. "No doubt I have to hear about it. What did you do?"

"When I was a senior I met this really beautiful townie and we started dating. Then some football player at her high school started cutting in and it pissed me off."

"I can't see a guy your size duking it out with most football players so I ask again, what did you do?"

"The girl's dad drove a school bus for Middletown. So I waited until one night when I knew she had a date with this jock. I went to the drug store and bought a pack of rubbers and sent a friend to the grocery store to buy a few eggs. We took the white of one egg and put it in a rubber, then pried open the door of the school bus and pitched it in.

"When the girl's old man got in the bus early the next morning and saw that rubber, he put two and two together and goodbye football player."

Taylor laughed. Even if he never had been one to play that kind of trick himself, he admired Welch for spicing up his life with the practical jokes.

"Well, Wheties, I also had myself a little fun before I came down today."

"I wondered where you were late this afternoon," said Welch. "Didn't see you around anywhere."

"I told you the other day I'd had enough of those Navy jerks holding reveille on us at Wheeler, so I went over to Bellows Field to see what was happening. That was just an excuse to be somewhere in that vicinity. What I really did was check out what was happening with the sailors and marines at the Kaneohe Naval Air Station. Things were quiet so I circled around and then went down and made a pass over at about 100 feet. Those swabbies were hitting the deck right and left. Maybe I didn't wake anybody up, but by god I got their attention."

"And what if they saw that big one five five on the side of your ship and call the old man?

"I wish they would," said Taylor, laughing. "The captain knows about their little Sunday morning flights over Wheeler, and I can imagine what he might have to say to some what you call 'Mr. Ice Cream Suit' Navy guy calling to complain about me."

Sitting at the bar over two Buds, the conversation came to their training and what they would do once in aerial combat, strafing or other fighter pilot functions such as escorting bombers.

While the self-confidence within Taylor and Welch might well have transcended that of all the other pilots in the 47th, both also had doubts.

"What worries me," Welch admitted, "is the learning curve once we get into combat whether in England, the

Philippines or other islands nobody ever heard of. I don't want to be killed up there, shot down over the English Channel or some place and maybe worst of all, being taken as a prisoner of war."

"Well, halleluiah, George, you got any other of those optimistic thoughts you want to share with me?"

"What I fear most is being a POW," said Welch, looking serious. "There already are horror stories going around about both the Nazis and the Japs and their concentration camps. They will never take me alive if there is any way I can kill myself to avoid it. So my plan is to never get in that situation if I can help it."

"I got my concerns, too."

"And what would they be."

"They be," answered Taylor, "having to take on guys who have had a bunch of experience in aerial combat. You and I have been a little creative in our mock dogfights just since we got here. Think about what those Nazi and Jap pilots have learned to survive. And we know the Zero and Messerschmitt 109 are faster and can outperform our ships, good as they are."

"Fast isn't everything," said Welch. "It helps but so does the armor that gives us protection and the self-sealing fuel tanks they don't have. But I think the real answer to beating those bastards is being creative with whatever planes they give us to fly."

He asked the bartender to bring two more beers and nudged Taylor in the ribs indicating it was his turn to buy.

"Why you so scared about being captured?"

"Being penned up," said Welch. "That's why I wanted to be a pilot. The wild blue yonder. You just think about it, Grits."

At that point Irv Henze, another 47th pilot walked up to where Ken and George were sitting and ordered a gin and tonic.

"Mind if I join you?"

"Of course not," said Welch.

Taylor turned on his bar stool to face Henze.

"Irv," he said, "you're a smart guy. What the hell do you think about our chances when we meet up with the Germans and Japs? In the air, I mean."

Henze reached over for his cocktail from the bartender and took a drink.

"This is what I think. When Capt. Austin was giving us that pep talk early this week, which we damned sure needed, he compared our focus in the air to basketball and football. But you know what he didn't mention, guys, and maybe on purpose?"

Taylor and Welch shrugged their ignorance.

"What the captain didn't say," Henze continued, "is that if you are going to compare our flying to sports, how would you bet on a football team that had been playing together for several years to one that had only practiced and never played a game?"

"Jesus Christ, Irv," said Welch. "You sure know how to get to the point"

"Yeah, and that's one point I'd just as soon not think about," said Taylor.

"Me either," said Henze, a pleasant man, looking down at the piece of lime floating in his drink. "I think the captain went as far as he should have gone with that sports analogy.

"We are a team, sure. But what we hear from the RAF is in the Brits' experience their boys, or 'lads' as they call them, work best in pairs.

"So we go out with our 25 planes in a "V" formation, and then all of a sudden there are Japs coming at us from every direction. At that point it's every man for himself except in those cases where he can help his wingman or another buddy in trouble. So much for a sports team strategy in a dogfight."

"We do have a doggone good plane," said Taylor.

"That's true," said Welch. "The P-40 has a good engine and some armor. It dives good and does well at low altitudes. I like that old bird."

Ken Taylor had ordered a cigar from the bartender. As he listened to his fellow pilots he bit off one end of the cigar and lit it.

"You know, fellers, we have a saying back in Oklahoma that you dance with the one who brung you. The P-40 is what will brung us to wherever we get into combat so we might as well be happy that we have it to dance with.

"Now it's Friday and we're off for the weekend so why don't we just have another round."

Current events of that day: The Aztec Clipper plane arriving in Honolulu from the coast included John Montgomery. Passengers going on to Manila included U. Saw, prime minister of Burma. A railroad strike threat faded when five operat-

ing brotherhoods of railroad employees ratified a wage agreement. Japanese troops were concentrated on the Thai front. A new post office was approved for Waikiki. Pitcher Bob Feller of the Cleveland Indians was making plans to join the Army or Navy. The American Automobile Association in Washington, DC announced plans for the longest auto race in history from the U.S. to Argentina.

December 6, 1941

"The Hickam Officers' Club was filled with the usual Saturday night crowd. Lieutenant Gray and 1st Lt. Donovan D. Smart finally received the white coats they had ordered from The Hub, a men's store in downtown Honolulu, so they got dates, rented a car, and attended a dinner-dance at the club. Captain and Mrs. Waldron and probably three-fourths of the pilots who were officers were also there at a big party. The waitresses were, ironically, clad in colorful Japanese Kimonos. A good time was had by all, and it was not until the early hours of the morning that the partygoers finally left to go home, looking forward to sleeping late that Sunday morning, 7 December 1941."

—"7 December 1941 The Air Force Story," p. 38.

While the sun obviously rises later and sets earlier in December in Hawaii, the length of the day hardly is noticeable for residents and tourists. On most days there is sunshine although occasionally it may be raining or partly cloudy.

But it's still warm over most of the island depending on the amount of wind and the direction from which it comes. Wheeler Field in its location in the central part of Oahu can be several degrees cooler than it is at Waikiki Beach.

All around the island the Pacific Ocean surf moves endlessly in a surge against sandy beaches and rocky cliffs as the tide goes in and goes out, while surfers wait for a wave big enough to justify their paddling out to where the breakers begin.

Weekends on the Army bases for those military personnel not on duty was not that much different than for civilians. It was time for washing clothes and cars, shopping, playing sports or just catching up on sleep.

Even in early December the sun would still be bringing tropical warmness to the Hawaiian Islands before the giant orange ball would slowly disappear over the dark green grass in the large area of Wheeler Field.

At 4 p.m. on Saturday George Welch was standing by the Taylor Buick in the parking area near the Bachelor Officers Quarters and Wheeler Field Officers' Club, leaning against the car smoking.

He was dressed in black tie with a black jacket and pants, his good looks enhanced by the formal dress.

Then Ken Taylor appeared dressed in black tie but with a white dinner jacket, cigarette in hand and the little "I know something you don't know" look on his face.

He opened the door on the left side and slid in, rolling down the window as he settled into the driver's seat.

Welch had gotten in on the passenger side and was flicking the ash off his Camel with his arm outside the window.

"You know, Grits," said Welch as Taylor put the car in gear and headed for the Wheeler guard gate, "back in Purdue they taught us that white dinner jackets aren't worn after the first of September. I don't understand why you keep wearing one now it's December."

"Because," said Taylor, "this is not Purdue and we are not in Indiana where it's probably so cold now it would freeze the balls off of a brass monkey. Out here it's summer all year around and I can't see the need to go buy a black jacket just because that's what you prefer."

"Your only saving grace," said Welch, "is that there are a few other inappropriately dressed guys, probably Navy, we'll be seeing tonight who are as ignorant or thrifty as you are wearing the same jacket you have on."

"Well, Wheaties, that reminds me of a little story one of the other pilots told me the other day."

"What was that?"

"It was about a thrifty cat."

"What about a thrifty cat?"

"Oh," said Taylor, "the thrifty cat put a little in the kitty every day. And I may be thrifty but unlike you I'm not putting anything in a kitty very often."

As the Buick traveled down the two-lane road toward Honolulu from Wheeler in the twilight, there could be seen the plush green pineapple plants in the red dirt fields on each side of the road and palm trees here and there.

For Taylor, getting duty in Hawaii was about as close to paradise as he could imagine it to be, a place where pineapples and bananas grew among the plush greenness of the island as opposed to the much barer land of Oklahoma where cotton and wheat were the major crops.

His home state of Oklahoma had just gone through years of the Dust Bowl era combined with the Great Depression. While his own small family had weathered those years without great hardship, from the stories he heard at home and on the WKY radio station in Oklahoma City and read in the Daily Oklahoman and Tulsa World he knew plenty about what people in his state had suffered.

If all these problems were not sufficient cause for despair back home, while he was at the University of Oklahoma the state had been hit by a tornado of negative publicity from John Steinbeck's best-selling book, "The Grapes of Wrath."

In the book a destitute Oklahoma family bought into the myth being spread around by fliers and word of mouth that jobs were plentiful in California, so off it went to the "Promised Land."

Steinbeck's book did expose the outrageous working conditions in California's Central Valley agricultural area, sometimes called "America's Breadbasket."

But for many another message from the book was perceived to be that the suffering would not have happened had the "Okies"—the all-encompassing term for those who headed west from various states—had just stayed home.

One of Oklahoma's congressmen, Lyle Boren, took to the House of Representatives floor on Jan. 23, 1940 and said, "I cannot find it possible to let this dirty, lying, filthy manuscript go heralded before the public without a word of challenge or protest."

Also in Washington, Rep. William J. Driver of Arkansas called Steinbeck's book "the greatest accumulation of filth ever published, and it ought to be suppressed."

Taylor did not let the "Okie" ribbing he had encountered since joining the Air Corps get under his skin. He had been born and reared in Oklahoma so there was not much he could do about his past, and if others viewed him as a lesser person he felt that was their problem and not his.

"We still going to the Royal Hawaiian?" asked Welch as they neared the outskirts of Honolulu.

"Yep. And you know what, if I get really lucky in a poker game some day I am coming down here to party all night when I can afford to stay over in the hotel."

"You ever try surfing?"

"No," replied Taylor. "We don't have a lot of water in Oklahoma and it's just not something that's ever attracted me much since I've been out here. Looks like a lot of work for a short ride."

"Looks like a helluva lot of fun to me."

"Then George, why don't we just come back down here tomorrow and you can try surfing while I try picking up a gal on the beach, or at least get my kicks looking at them."

"Going to the beach is nothing new to me," said Welch. "We've got great, unspoiled beaches in Delaware. Lewes, Rehoboth and Bethany aren't that far from Wilmington and in the summers it was a great place to pick up girls on weekends. Or we would drive on down a ways to Ocean City, Maryland, which was always crawling with women."

"I didn't know Delaware had beaches," said Taylor. "You must have had all the poontang you could take care of," said Taylor.

"I did okay," said Welch. "But for some reason it always embarrassed me to go in a drug store to buy rubbers."

"Maybe if we come to Waikiki tomorrow we'll get to see Duke Kahanamoku," said Taylor.

"Duke who?"

"Duke Kahanamoku, the great Olympic swimmer and surfer. He's the sheriff here now. Maybe if you had told that cop who nailed your ass that you knew Duke he wouldn't have given you a ticket."

"Oh, unlike my brilliant buddy I did not know that Duke's last name. Hell, I'd go to jail if I could see the great Duke. But unless somebody is making a movie or paying him, I doubt we would ever be seeing Duke surfing at Waikiki."

"So maybe as a consolation you could get an autograph from that Navy brass guy in the ice cream suit when you pulled your little parachute trick last week. His rank is equal to a full bird in the Army so he's no doubt a big shot out here."

"Screw you, Grits."

As the Buick made it's way easily through the Waikiki area of Honolulu the bright street lights showed sailors in their white, bell bottom trouser uniforms, soldiers and marines in their khakis and a mixture of locals and tourists who had come from the mainland on cruise ships.

A popular spot mostly for enlisted men was the Black Cat Café across from the YMCA.

The two pilots had stopped in one weekend while in civilian clothes.

Being the "thrifty cat" Welch had dubbed him on the drive from Wheeler, Taylor took to the Black Cat Café the minute he looked at the menu.

Cheeseburgers were twenty cents, Cokes a nickel with meals and fried chicken, a Taylor favorite, sixty cents.

"This is my kind of place," said Taylor, ordering fried chicken with vegetables and strawberry short cake.

"Wait a minute, Grits, I think you made a mistake there."

"How's that?" asked Taylor, putting down the menu.

"Hell, right here on my menu it says "Pig's feet. And only twenty cents. How you letting a good old Okie meal go by, especially since it's less than a quarter?"

Taylor got the little smirk on his face. He liked Welch's ribbing. But because the Black Cat did not serve liquor they never went there again.

Taylor lucked out and found a parking place for the Buick on Kalakaua Avenue about a hundred yards from the entrance to the pink edifice of the Royal Hawaiian.

At the hotel, they walked through the lobby to the small manicured grass and palm tree area separating the rear of the building from the sandy beach. From there they could hear the soft roar of the surf and smell the special odor of the pristine ocean.

On a small wooden stage a three-piece Hawaiian band played while a young woman dressed in a sarong gracefully danced the hula.

Surrounding the stage and a small bar were folding wood chairs made from the darkly stained banyan trees with pink seat covers, the theme color of the grand old hotel. Hardly had they sat down when a lovely young

Hawaiian female walking barefooted on the sand appeared to take their orders for drinks.

Taylor ordered a gin and tonic and Welch a rum drink garnished with slices of pineapple and maraschino cherries.

Generally both pilots drank beer because it was cheap, and limited their party routine to the officers' clubs where all drinks and food were much less expensive than in Honolulu bars and restaurants.

The drink orders arrived promptly and both men sat listening to the music while watching the lights from the hotel reflected on the phosphorous of the white-capped waves washing up on the sand.

Taylor took a sip of his drink and set it down on the little table that separated his chair from Welch's.

"You know, George, I don't hear much from my university brethren back in Oklahoma, but if they could see us sitting here tonight they would think we were the luckiest two sonofabitches in the world."

Welch removed the little umbrella from his drink and took a long swig, smacking his lips at the sweet taste.

"I doubt they would be thinking that at all."

Taylor, his white jacket unbuttoned, turned to his friend.

"Why the hell would they not be wishing they were in our shoes sitting here in a place like this?"

Welch finished his drink and waved at the waitress to bring another.

"So you're a gambler, Kenny boy. Well, I'll give you ten to one that a month from now there will be Army troops patrolling this beach and we will be the hell and gone somewhere getting our asses shot off by Japs or

Germans. And the boys back at Purdue and Oklahoma will be crawling around in mud taking basic training on some Army base in a swamp in Louisiana."

Taylor had lit a cigar and was sipping his gin and tonic.

"From what I read and hear on the radio I think I'd prefer the Germans. They know how to make good machinery. They're mean as hell and by now have had a helluva lot of combat experience."

"Just be careful where you go with that German stuff. I'm German."

Taylor looked at Welch, not knowing if he was serious or joking.

"If a guy named Welch is German, then I must be St. Patrick."

"My name was changed when I was born. It was Schwartz, which still is my middle name, but my mother was a Welch so I became one. It's all because of what my folks along with a lot of other German-Americans went through in that war to end all wars. And I think it was a good move."

Taylor laughed.

"So we both know something about discrimination."

"No, not for me like you say it is with you and the other Okies. I missed that by being named Welch. But I appreciate the compliment about Germans in general in your offhand remarks that started this conversation."

One hula dancer had left the little stage to be replaced by another, equally beautiful and graceful in a blue and white flowered muu muu enhancing her ethnic tanned color.

Behind her the three Hawaiian men were playing a ukulele, guitar and bass. They were dressed in white dinner jackets with red bow ties and purple orchids pinned on the lapels.

Welch had finished a second drink and signaled for the waitress to bring another.

Taylor took a puff on his cigar and looked at his buddy.

"Are you really enjoying those drinks or just the sight of the waitress' breasts when she bends over to put the glass on the table?"

"I'm enjoying everything because I think this 'just another day in paradise,' shave-tail's fantasy duty may be about to go bye, bye. But please excuse me because I got to go take a piss."

Back in the Royal Hawaiian lobby, Welch asked to use the phone near the check in desk and requested the operator to get him the surgical ward at the Tripler Army Hospital.

"Surgical ward, may I help you?" came a female voice when the call had been put through.

"Uh, well, sorry to bother you but could I please speak to Miss Nightingale?"

"Just a minute," said the woman who answered. "She's just down the hall. I'll get her."

"Hello," soon came another female voice, "This is Miss Nightingale. Can I help you?"

'Hey, Flo, this is George. How's it going?"

"Oh, George, how you doing? I was just making the evening rounds. Where are you?"

"My buddy Ken Taylor and I are down at the Royal Hawaiian getting shitfaced. Guess we'll probably hit Hickam before we have a nightcap or two at the Wheeler club."

"Darn, I'd love to be down there with you. But as you know the new second lieutenants get the short end of the stick with weekend and night duty."

"Uh, Flo, how's about we get together Monday night. You're off then, right?"

"I'd love to," said Flo, "but we can't do your BOQ thing again. If we get caught they'll kick us out of the Army and I kinda like it out here."

"Then why don't we meet at the club over at Shafter? Have dinner, some drinks, you know…"

"George, that's okay with me but we can't go back to my place either because I have a roommate and I don't think she's into voyeurism."

"Okay, okay," said Welch, feeling the effects of the rum drinks. "I'll borrow Taylor's car and meet you at the club around five o'clock. Okay?"

"Okay," came the cheery reply. "See you then and have fun tonight."

When Welch returned to the beach a few couples were dancing but the crowd had thinned.

"Well, Wheaties, I don't see much action here. Might as well head out for Hickham."

"Yeah," said Welch. "I'm ready for some dinner and no doubt there will be some nurses or daughters of officers we can grab for a few dances."

Taylor picked up his cigar from the ashtray on the little table that separated their chairs and started to leave.

"Grits, hold on. There's this little matter of paying the check."

"Oh, that," said Taylor, reaching for his wallet. "I figured you were taking care of it since you were ordering all those fancy drinks."

The Hickam Field Officers' Club was swinging when Taylor and Welch arrived there after the drive from the Royal Hawaiian Hotel on Waikiki Beach.

Most of the tables were filled with officers ranging from those with a wife or date dining alone at a table to some groups where as many as a dozen sat together. The combination odor of liquor, cigarettes and various dishes of food was in sharp contrast to the December night air the two pilots had enjoyed driving over from Waikiki.

A twelve-piece orchestra, all men and dressed in flowery Hawaiian shirts and white trousers, were playing popular songs and the dance floor was covered with couples dancing close together to the tune of the Andrews Sisters big hit, "I'll Be with You in Apple Blossom Time."

The maitre de found a table for two and escorted the pilots to where they were seated in the hazy, smoke-filled air close to the dance floor.

"George, what the hell are you staring at?" asked Taylor as they sat down.

"Just checking out the bar and there's no action there so we might as well eat."

"Why didn't you get a date with that nurse you slept with the other night?"

"She has weekend duty. I called her from the Royal Hawaiian and we're going out Monday night. And I might ask why you aren't out with Miss Oklahoma?"

"I told you once," said Taylor. "I don't think we're real compatible just because we're both from Oklahoma."

"What was her name, something kind of different wasn't it?"

"It's Flora Love."

"Flora Love?"

"Yes, Flora Love. I guess I'll try seeing her again one of these days. Tell you something, she's not only a real cutie but smart as hell."

"No dumb blonde, huh?"

Welch's question already had been answered, and a waitress dressed in a Japanese kimono with the faint smell of the fresh flowers, emanating from the lei around her neck, appeared to take their order. Both chose steaks and the same thing they had been drinking at the Royal Hawaiian.

They lit cigarettes and listened to the music until their drinks came.

"George, I was just thinking. Why don't we see if I can get Flora Love and you get your nurse and we'll go to the Royal Hawaiian for Christmas dinner. I imagine short of us being in a war somewhere by then that would be a nice thing to do."

"See, I think you've been pulling my leg about Flora Love and you having doubts about getting along together. C'mon, Grits, why not admit it?

"Well my real concern is about being hooked up with a gal who is a lot smarter than I am."

"Yeah, man," laughed Welch. "That bothers me too. Had some experiences with that back in Purdue."

Then the waitress was at their table with their steaks and the two pilots were mostly silent as they watched the action in the club as they ate.

Dressed in the required black tie, it was not possible to tell who was in which service or a man's rank but obviously older men were higher up the ladder.

As the band played such numbers as "Beer Barrel Polka," "Blue Berry Hill" and "Oh Johnny, Oh Johnny, Oh!" a scattering of usually younger couples would be on the dance floor jitterbugging. When the band played slower tunes such as "All the Things You Are," "You and I" and "White Cliffs of Dover," so many couples would get up to dance there was hardly room to move.

Welch, the more mischievous and adventurous of the two, stubbed out his cigarette and turned to his friend.

"You know, Kenny boy, all those women out there dancing aren't necessarily either married or engaged. Why don't we pick us a couple of cuties and ask if we can cut in?"

"Good idea," said Taylor, standing and both pilots walked the short distance to the dance floor.

While eating each had been checking out the most attractive of the women who also danced well. In the crush on the floor to a slow dance both tapped shoulders of male partners and politely asked if they might cut in. Both men looked surprised but as officers and gentlemen they left the ladies and went back to their tables.

Taylor, who had first learned to dance at the Acacia fraternity at the University of Oklahoma, moved rather smoothly holding a beautiful brunette, dimpled cheeks and a ready smile.

"I'm Ken."

"Hi, Ken, I'm Mimi. You're a smooth dancer."

"Thanks, Mimi," said Taylor, "I see you're wearing a ring. What's your husband do out here?"

"Jack's a Navy pilot. He's supposed to be out with Adm. Halsey's task force on the Enterprise, one of the Navy carriers, but he has some kind of eye problem so they left him at Pearl. What do you do, Ken?"

"I'm just an old Army pilot. The problem with my eyes is I can't keep them off you."

"Oh, aren't you sweet. Are you here at Hickam?"

"Nope, my buddy and I are over at Wheeler. We been down on Waikiki and thought we'd stop in here and eat."

"I work here at Hickam in personnel. Jack will be going back to sea in two weeks, so why don't you give me a call?

For all his country boy audacity, Taylor missed a beat with his feet from the surprise invitation from Mimi.

"A call, uh, where do I give you a call?"

"Here," said Mimi. "In personnel. Everybody knows me so all you have to do is ask for Mimi."

"Then maybe I will," said Taylor.

With the song ended, Taylor and Welch escorted their partners back to their table of four couples and all the men stood as the women arrived.

"How'd it go?" asked Welch.

"Oh, she's a fine dancer. Married to a swabbie pilot. Nice lady."

"My partner's husband's also a Navy pilot, probably from the same squadron."

"Probably," said Taylor. "We didn't talk about that much."

As Welch lit a cigarette he leaned over the table.

"You've got that little smirk on your face like the cat that swallowed the canary. So what the hell are you holding out on me?" And he blew smoke right into his friend's face.

Before Taylor could respond, both he and Welch heard a "harrumph" and realized someone was standing by their table. When they turned to see who was there, both stood more or less at attention since they were facing a tall, very tanned man a few years older than the two of them.

"Yessir," said Welch. "Can we help you?"

"You can help yourselves," said the man, looking from Welch to Taylor, "but you cannot help yourselves to the women at my table. I'm Capt. Waldron, 31st Squadron, and if you want dancing partners at this club then I would suggest you gentlemen bring your own the next time."

"Well, sir," drawled Taylor, "we was just here by ourselves and out in the country where I come from it ain't no harm to dance with another feller's woman."

"We are not out in the country in Arkansas or wherever you come from. We are in an officers' club in Hawaii. So I would strongly suggest that if you gentlemen want to dance, the next time bring someone to dance with. Understood?"

"YESSIR," the two pilots said simultaneously as they gave their usual poor excuse for a salute.

Waldron flipped them a neat salute, nodded and turned to go.

"Jesus, Grits, what the hell did you do to that gal, pinch her on the ass?"

"I was a perfect gentleman and I had the feeling the young woman enjoyed the dance, and maybe that's the reason that feller is so pissed off."

Welch looked at Taylor shaking his head.

"I thought you said the girl you danced with was a Navy wife and that guy who's so upset is with the Air Corps 31st. You mean our guys are fraternizing with the Navy?"

"I don't know," said Taylor. "Maybe they're neighbors or went to the same college or something like that. Whatever the situation, he sure did have a bee in his bonnet."

"One of these days," said Welch, "somebody is going to call you on your country yokel act, and your wings are going to fly away as you start living in a foxhole with the ground troops."

"Could be, but as my old man used to say, 'You got to know when to hold 'em and know when to fold 'em.'"

It was now after 1 a.m. on Dec. 7, the orchestra had played its last song and the musicians were packing up their instruments. Checks were being paid with chits and not cash as the elegantly dressed diners and party people were leaving.

"Guess it's time to be heading back to the base," said Welch.

"Done here," Taylor agreed.

Little was said as the two pilots rode with windows rolled down and cigarette smoke trailing out of the red Buick in the cool night on the ride from Hickam Field to Wheeler.

"You ready to hit the sack?" asked Welch.

"Both of us already have had enough to drink for a weekend," replied Taylor. "But, I think if the club is still open we should have ourselves one of those fancy brandy drinks as a nightcap and who knows, there might still be a poker game going on."

"Sounds good to me," said Welch. "But don't come waking me up for breakfast in the morning. I'm thinking I'll sleep until at least noon chow, maybe later."

"It's been a good week," said Taylor. "Damn but I loved shooting at that flag target but I would sure like to get the feel of firing my .50s as well as the 30s. And I reckon next week we'll be doing our strafing over at Bellows Field. We need practice on what the captain has been telling us for months. You gotta get an air speed of at least two hundred miles an hour to get the P-40s nose down to where you can aim and shoot."

"I know," said Welch, "they told us why the gun sights were set just off to the right instead of dead center in front of the cockpit. But all of a sudden when I was drawing a bead on the flag target it all made sense."

By then Taylor had parked the Buick in front of the club and the two were getting out not even bothering to roll up the windows.

"Damn good ship, that old P-40," said Welch.

Inside the Wheeler Officers' Club the crowd consisted of a bartender both pilots recognized as a mechanic in the 47th squadron and four tux-clad men playing poker off in one corner.

Taylor and Welch got drinks at the bar and wandered over to the poker game.

"New blood," said a second lieutenant named Ed Tighe, looking up. With him was another 47th pilot named

John Dains. He introduced the other players. One was a tall, blond pilot named Rasmussen from another squadron and the fourth a maintenance officer for the base.

"Rasmussen is still flying a P-36," said Tighe, studying his cards. "Tell our squadron hotshots how it is to fly one of those older crates."

Rasmussen did not respond immediately as he concentrated on the game.

"The P-36 doesn't have all the upgrades of the P-40," he finally said. "But I don't feel like an orphan flying it, good old ship as far as I'm concerned."

Welch went back to the bar for two more drinks. He and Taylor sat and watched the action but with none of the players indicating he was going to quit the game they agreed to hit the sack.

It had been a good evening very much justifying the decision of both pilots when they requested fighters and duty in Hawaii.

As they walked from the club the short distance to their quarters Taylor thought he might in the next few days tell his friend about the come on from the married Navy wife. Ken Taylor was no puritan, but somehow it did not seem right in his mind to be messing around with a married woman, no matter how attractive she was, when her old man was at sea. But as he said goodnight to Welch and each headed for different buildings of the Wheeler bachelor officers quarters, Taylor could not forget Mimi's dimples, smile and flattering invitation to have an affair when her husband was away.

He looked at his watch as he walked into the dimly lighted lanai at the entrance to the building where the sole telephone was mounted on one side of the door to the corridor separating the two rows of rooms. It was 3 a.m.

It was doubtful either Taylor or Welch or anybody at the military installations in Hawaii had even dreamed that morning would be the beginning of one of the most fateful days in the country's history.

Current events of that day*: Hirohito Holds Power To Stop Japanese Army (headline). Actor Jackie Cooper's mother died in Hollywood. Miss Barbara Alden Dow married Ensign Jack Dalton Martin at the home of the bride's parents in Kahawai. Rear Adm. Richard Byrd in a radio speech from New York urged United States employers to end religious and racial bias. In Chicago a group of world leaders including British Ambassador Hallifax outlined their own views on a lasting world peace. The Navy announced in Washington, DC it was starting construction on a 150-bed hospital in Key West, Fla. The world's largest aircraft, the B-19 bomber, completed six months of tests and the Army accepted the plane from the Douglas plant in Santa Monica, Cal.*

December 7, 1941

"I think we can meet with confidence all threats of enemy encroachment even that of bombardment from the air."

Lt. Gen. Walter C. Short, USA, during a radio speech given on May 20, 1941, to the people of the Territory of Hawaii.

—"7 December 1941 The Air Force Story," p. 1.

The noise that awoke Ken Taylor just before 8 a.m. Sunday morning was not unusual. Some Navy pilot smartass, he assumed, was at it again holding reveille on the Wheeler Field personnel knowing most of them had the weekend off and could sleep in.

As Taylor rolled over to go back to sleep, there was a very loud, vibrating explosion.

Stupid swabbie, thought Taylor as he sat up and put his feet on the floor. He's gone off the main route somewhere here on the base.

The closest trousers were the tux pants, so he pulled them on along with shoes and a tux shirt to go see where the Navy pilot had crashed and no doubt lost his life. And for what, just to play a little "wake up" game with the Army boys.

Running down the hallway of the BOQ through the lanai to the street, Taylor was stunned to see aircraft flying over him with the Japanese red "meatball" painted on the gray fuselages. Out on the ramp he could see black smoke and bright red flames rising high from the Wheeler aircraft lined up wing tip to wing tip on the ramp as Gen. Short had ordered over the objections of Col. Flood, Wheeler commander.

Men were running from various buildings and some were being riddled with bullets from the rear gunner of the Japanese planes as they made their passes over the field.

"Grits, what the hell is going on? Those sonofabitches are bombing the hell out of us!"

Taylor looked around to see George Welch standing near him in the middle of the street. It was hard to hear what Welch was saying for the noise of the bombs and the machine gun fire from the Japanese planes–low enough overhead they could see the smiling faces of the pilots.

Taylor reached in his tux pants pockets and came out holding the keys to his Buick, which he pitched to Welch.

"Get my car, George," he yelled to be heard over the chaotic scene. "I'll call Haleiwa and tell them to get some planes ready!"

Welch took off for the parking lot as Taylor ran back to the BOQ lanai. Just as he reached for the old phone near the door to the hallway, a stream of bullets from one of the Japanese planes went by him and on down the hallway separating the rooms on each side.

Someone, probably the Italian corporal, answered the phone at Haleiwa and Taylor conveyed the order in a loud voice to get two P-40s ready because he and Welch would soon be there.

Running to the red Buick, Taylor smelled the unique odor of black smoke from aviation fuel and listened to severely wounded men screaming for help off near the mess hall.

As Welch drove the Buick out through the Wheeler gate without even slowing and headed toward Haleiwa, Taylor punched in the lighter on the dash and lit two Luckys. He handed one to Welch and took a deep drag from his own.

"These may be our last cigarettes," yelled Taylor over the noise of the engine, air rushing through the window and the tires speedily scratching along on the unpaved road.

At some point early on during the ten-mile ride the two young pilots heard the pop pop of bullets passing from a low-flying Japanese plane firing at them.

"Give it all it's got, George," yelled Taylor at the driver. "But just don't get it in a ditch."

Welch had good control of the Buick and in not many minutes he was braking it to a stop in front of the 47th Squadron's planes on the PCP ramp back near the tents.

The ground crew helped the two pilots don their yellow life jackets and get buckled in with helmets pulled on, the goggles raised above their foreheads. Everyone around them was taking an occasional glance at the sky, expecting an attack on the field at any moment.

With a quick "chunk, chunk, chunk" the two P-40 engines started and the pilots headed down the oceanside runway with light brown sand flying from their prop wash.

Both Taylor and Welch had seen Lt. Rogers arrive, but under the circumstances saw no reason to wait for his orders considering the Japs were up there unopposed bombing and shooting hell out of everything back at Wheeler.

Ground crews were rolling out more of the squadron's planes for other pilots who might be showing up to join Taylor and Welch in repulsing the surprise attack.

Two crew chiefs, both sergeants, stood with hands on hips watching the Taylor and Welch planes leave the runway and head briefly out over the water before making a turn back toward Wheeler and the action there.

"That wop corporal in the headquarters tent says they're pounding the shit out of Wheeler," said one of the sergeants. "Really bad over there."

"Then what the hell are we doing standing here with our heads up our asses?" asked the other sergeant. "Man, we don't even have foxholes to get in if they come here. Come on, let's find shovels and start digging."

Within minutes Taylor and Welch had gained altitude and headed toward Wheeler.

"Ops," Taylor called on his radio. "Taylor and Welch up here just leaving Haleiwa. What's happening over there now?"

Kermit Tyler, the first lieutenant on duty, calmly took the microphone.

"You know as much as I do, boys. We're at war with the Japs and our building has even taken a hit."

Moments later the two pilots were approaching Wheeler with the dark smoke clouds now boiling up several hundred feet high in the sky from the bombed and strafed planes on the ramp. But not an enemy plane was in sight.

On the ground at Wheeler men could be seen moving as ants, running here and there to fight fires burning hangars and, worst of all, the incredible sight of planes from various squadrons as the source of a massive fire where they had been parked wing tip to wing tip.

"Holy Christ," said Taylor. "Look down there. Hell, all they've got left for planes is the 47th!"

The carnage at Wheeler as the P-40s gained air speed and altitude was only a momentary distraction for the two pilots, who had not forgotten the number of planes they had seen attacking Wheeler as they stood on the streets between the two BOQ buildings after being awakened by the noise.

Somewhere up there were the Japanese planes that had attacked Wheeler and probably many more, and to shoot some down and survive was by far the major focus for Taylor and Welch as Capt. Austin had forewarned.

"Hey, Grits," yelled Welch on his radio. "Look over there. Whole string of 'em!"

As the two pilots approached from high above the dozen planes their thumbs moved over the firing button on the sticks, excitement swelling up as they prepared to shoot at their first enemy aircraft.

"Hold your horses, Wheaties," yelled Taylor. "Those are B-17s. Must be coming in from the mainland."

Both P-40s banked and were now approaching an air speed of 300 MPH at an altitude of 10,000 feet as they headed toward Pearl Harbor, knowing it was their job to protect the ships anchored there.

Far in the distance Welch spotted a line of dots on the horizon across the island near the Marine base at Ewa.

"Hey, buddy," called Welch. "Get your thumb on the button because I see Jap bombers down there just like sitting ducks."

From their position just past Wheeler it appeared there might be as many as a dozen Japanese planes probably eight to ten miles away and a good thousand feet below them. From that distance they appeared to be Japanese dive bombers with a pilot and rear gunner.

With an air speed now nearing 345 MPH they soon would be there. The fingers of both Taylor and Welch moved over the firing button on their sticks as they prepared to dive on the unsuspecting bombers.

"Well, good luck, pard," said Taylor and there was silence from the other P-40.

Then on the radio from Welch.

"I'm taking the last one in the line." You get the plane in front of him."

As both pilots put their planes into dives picking up more air speed, the closer they came they easily recognized the enemy aircraft as dive bombers, probably headed to Pearl Harbor to attack the ships anchored there.

Both Taylor and Welch put their targets in their gun sights and led them slightly so their fire would start near the pilot's position in the cockpit and run back to disable the rear gunner.

Welch pushed his firing button first and watched as the red tracers spaced along the belt of bullets went true to the front of the cockpit and Taylor's fire did the same to the plane that was his target. The two Americans roared past the line of bombers and did an arching inside loop from where they could see both their targets peel off in flames, trailing black smoke as they headed earthward.

At an altitude of 13,000 feet the two P-40s came sweeping down with .30 calibers firing all the way and two more dive bombers started spouting flames out of control with dead pilots at the controls.

"Grits," Welch yelled on the radio," I'm flat ass out of ammo and I think one of my guns is jammed. Heading to Wheeler. Give me some cover, will ya?"

"Roger," called Taylor. "I still got some rounds and I got your ass covered so let's get going."

When Welch in minutes was approaching Wheeler with his nose down and full flaps to slow speed, the planes on the ramp were still burning. But Wheeler being one big area of grass, it was no problem to glide his P-40 to a landing with the wheels touching the greenness beneath the plane.

The scene at Wheeler was still total chaos, men and vehicles chasing around to fight fires, tending to the wounded and trying to mount some kind of defense by getting machines guns on the roofs of buildings. At some hangars ground crews were pushing planes that had been in a state of maintenance out of the hangars with pilots looking for anything that would fly.

Knowing the designated spot on the field for planes to be rearmed, by the time Welch's P-40 wheels were touching down ground crews with ammo carts were at the ready to service the aircraft as it was taxied to where they awaited with both .50 and .30 caliber ammo.

After Taylor landed he pulled his plane up near Welch's, and both pilots sat with their cockpit hatches pulled back feeling they would kill for a few puffs on a cigarette. Fortunately, the wind was blowing the smoke from the burning planes on the ramp, hangars and other buildings on fire in the opposite direction so they at least could breath some fresh air.

As soon as Welch had killed his engine a sergeant had run up to the plane to ask if he needed fuel.

"No fuel," Welch told him. "Just give me the ammo. These damned thirties are just one level above B.B. guns and one isn't even working but we're not taking the time to fix it now."

It seemed to him the ground crew was working too slow but he knew it was just his own anxiety about getting the ship up again. He didn't bother to look at his watch, figuring about an hour had passed since they jumped in the car and headed for Haleiwa.

Within a few minutes after Taylor's P-40 had stopped on the grassy side of what passed for a Wheeler runway two Air Corps ground crewmen had jumped up on the wings on each side of the cockpit with belts of ammunition.

One, Pvt. Stuart "Bud" Sweeney had a belt of .50 caliber and quickly opened the cowl to get access to the box that held the rounds for the two .50s that fired from the P-40s nose through the propeller. At the same time other crewmen with belts of .30 caliber were in the area of the wing guns to put new ammo in the receptacles there.

But there was a glitch. Sweeney asked Taylor if his prop had been synchronized to let the .50s fire through it. The question momentarily stunned the young pilot as he realized the sychronization had not happened because up to that time there had been no need for the more powerful rounds.

"Forget it," Taylor yelled at Sweeney." I'll do the best I can with the .30s."

As they sat waiting for the rearming to end, neither Taylor nor Welch was prepared for what happened next.

Behind the two P-40s and not in sight of the pilots, Gen. Davidson's staff car had pulled up and stopped. Out of the vehicle ran two majors, each jumping up on the wings of the planes to talk to the pilots.

"Just what the hell do you guys think you're doing?" asked the major on Taylor's wing.

"Well," replied Taylor, somewhat surprised by the question from a very much superior officer, "it looks like somebody started a war and Welch and I thought we might do what we could to stop it."

"Don't give me some damned smartass answer, lieutenant," snarled the major. "Who the hell told you guys to get in your planes and get up there anyhow? Capt. Austin is over on Molokai and we don't know where Lt. Rogers is. So the general says disperse your aircraft and don't even think about going up again. Understand, lieutenant?"

"Yessir," replied Taylor, giving the major a half-assed salute. "Just where should we disperse our ships?"

He had seen another officer jump up on Welch's left wing and assumed he was getting the same orders.

From the major's position standing on the wing dressing down Taylor, he could see across the field in the direction of Pearl Harbor. And what he saw was another flight of Japanese planes heading for a second attack on Wheeler.

The major on Welch's wing also heard and saw the Japanese planes heading toward the field. Both officers jumped off the planes and ran for shelter.

Welch, whose rearming was finished but the jammed .30 caliber gun not fixed, brought his right arm up and thrust it forward to indicate he was taking off. Pushing the throttle all the way forward, he rolled across the grass field and was soon airborne.

Taylor did not need Welch's leadership to make his decision to go up again. Screw the brass, he thought. *We are now in a war and I am not going to sit on my ass as a target here and let some Jap pilot finish me off.* The possibility of a court martial for disobeying orders under the circumstances did not even elicit a thought.

But Taylor had an urgent problem. Some members of the rearming crew, having seen the second group of Japanese attackers approaching, had scattered for cover and left the ammo cart in front of his left wing.

The development of this scenario was in seconds, not minutes. There was no time for him to jump out and move the cart. So he pushed his throttle forward and luckily the cart went careening off leaving him free to start his takeoff roll.

Pvt. Sweeney on one wing and the other ground crewman on the opposite side of the fuselage were given no warning and unceremoniously dumped on their backs in the grass as Taylor's P-40 lurched forward.

Sweeney and the other private quickly jumped to their feet and headed for the only cover available anywhere near.

That happened to be the large concrete base for one of the floodlights used to illuminate Wheeler for night flights. When they arrived there they were surprised to find they had company at this shelter at least against gunfire from the Japanese planes. Gen. Davidson and the two majors who were his aides as well as his driver also were crouched there.

Then two pieces of outrageous good luck for Taylor. Wheeler Field being grass, he did not have to taxi to a runway. Second, he could take off firing at the approaching Japanese planes, and the only way they could fire at him would be to fly into the ground. So off he went, guns blasting away.

Once airborne. Taylor pushed the throttle full forward and pulled back on the stick. The smoothly purring Allison engine took the plane almost straight up to the point Taylor wanted to pull out of the loop of the chandelle maneuver to level off.

As the day had warmed cloud cover had formed over the Wheeler area and all of a sudden Taylor found himself within a line of Japanese planes.

He had the airspeed necessary but before he could align his sights on the plane in front of him the unexpected happened.

From somewhere up above a Japanese Zero fighter pilot had spotted Taylor's P-40 and put it in his gunsights. Diving at an angle down on the P-40 the Zero started firing and a single bullet came through the cockpit canopy by Taylor's head with a loud bang, hit the half-grapefruit sized metal trim tab, went cleanly through Taylor's left arm then exploded at his feet sending a dozen sharp brass shards into his legs.

"Damn!" Taylor yelled, not at all sure of what had just happened. And immediately he forgot his targeting the Japanese plane almost in his sights and began to focus on how the hell he was going to get out of this mess quick. The bullet that came through the canopy probably was not more than an inch or two from his head. The arm wound was hardly a factor now. His single thought was how to save his plane and his life.

Shoving the throttle forward he pushed the stick to the left as far as he could go and felt his guts keep going straight ahead as he pulled the G forces of the abrupt turn.

Back behind him he heard the faint sound of machine guns firing and knew George was somewhere near enough to maybe get the Jap on his tail. During the left bank, this was confirmed as he saw a "meatball" plane heading downward with smoke trailing in its wake.

""You get him, George?"

"A Zero I think and he's finished."

"Where are they now? The line of meatballs I was in?"

"Keep banking left and follow me. Think they may be heading over towards Bellows."

Taylor did as told by his fellow flight leader.

The lower left sleeve of his khaki shirt was now near covered with blood from the elbow down and he noticed in a quick glance it was dripping on his tux pants. There was almost no pain in his left arm but it would not have mattered if it had hurt like hell.

He realized how stupid he had been as he gained altitude on the second flight, thinking there was not much to aerial combat if you really knew what you were doing.

Problem was he just thought he was better than the Jap pilots, which he now knew was not true.

Ever since they became airborne both Taylor and Welch had occasionally been searching the skies above Oahu for other American planes and had seen none.

Surely some of the other pilots in the 47th, 44th or other squadrons had been able to get off the ground. He and Welch had seen Lt. Rogers, the squadron operations officer; arrive at Haleiwa before they took off. But at the high rate of speed and searching the skies for the attackers there was no time to be picking out what was a P-40 or P-36 in the distance where he thought he could see two planes going at it.

Then both Taylor and Welch spotted the squadron of what appeared to be torpedo bombers below them and agreed on the same plan of attack used over Ewa.

Welch put his P-40 into a steep dive and almost instantly began sending a stream of bullets, their path clear by the red streak of intermittent tracer rounds, into the enemy plane's engine and back into the right wing housing a fuel tank.

The plane literally exploded with reddish yellow flames and pieces flying in all directions.

In a spilt second decision Taylor's deadly .30 calibers went right to the cockpit of the bomber that was his target and he could see the pilot slumped over as he passed by.

With a dead pilot the plane would eventually crash but Taylor wanted to make sure it went down right then, so he took his P-40 into a wide sweeping arc that brought it back on the Jap's tail. From a close distance to the rear his .30 calibers peppered the wing tanks and the ensuing fire from the fuel there put the plane into a spiraling dive.

Adm. Yamamoto's assignment for the fast, maneuverable Zeroes was to fly protection for the bombers but also to strafe where there was a target of opportunity.

Suddenly Taylor saw a Zero swoop past him with its guns firing. He knew he once again was having great luck that the Japanese pilot had misjudged the P-40's ability to bank, causing the enemy pilot to overshoot his target which was Taylor's plane with the big number "155" painted on its sides.

Kicking his right rudder pedal, moving the stick and pushing the throttle forward, Taylor followed the lighter and faster Japanese fighter on the chance he might get in a few rounds should the distance between the two planes be closed enough.

But then the Japanese pilot did the unexpected. He banked right, losing some of his air speed and putting himself right in Taylor's P-40 gunsights.

The enemy's maneuver was so unexpected, by the time Taylor could start firing his tracers showed him the bullets had only hit the other plane's tail in the rudder area where they did no harm.

Taylor swore and pulled back on the stick to shoot up a few thousand feet to check out not only where the Zero might be but also look for George's P-40 among the broken clouds.

In the far distance out over the water he could see Welch chasing a Zero that, while trailing no smoke, clearly was headed down into the water with the pilot most likely killed and fallen forward over the stick.

Quickly checking his left arm to see if the bleeding had stopped, Taylor broke through the clouds and saw what probably was a torpedo bomber a few hundred feet below and apparently heading back to its carrier.

Checking the air around him for Zeros flying cover, Taylor banked to the south for a few minutes then came back north toward Haleiwa where the Japanese bomber was still over land. With the plane in his sights, he led it by just a tad and then pushed the button that sent the deadly bullets from the red "meatball" painted on the side of the fuselage in a stream running on up to the engine.

As he sped by overhead Taylor did a chandelle and watched as the bomber headed almost straight down toward the ground.

Meanwhile, Welch had returned over land to search for any other enemy planes returning to their carriers.

By then both Taylor and Welch knew they were low on ammo and headed back to Haleiwa for orders on what they should do next. A new wave of Japanese planes coming over the island was not out of the possibility.

Welch had already pushed his canopy back and was crawling out of the cockpit when Taylor's P-40 pulled up beside his plane.

With his right hand Taylor pushed back his canopy and lifted himself up so he could ease out on the wing.

"Hey, Grits," yelled Welch, pointing to the blood-stained sleeve of his friend's shirt. "Now I know what it means when somebody's been winged."

"By God, I figured if I was going to fly around up there all morning I ought to at least get a Purple Heart out of it," Taylor retorted, jumping off the wing.

Welch thought his buddy looked a little pale from the wound and walked with him to the medical tent. En route, both pilots were surprised to see two of the B-17 bombers that had flown in from the States had chosen to land at Haleiwa apparently to avoid the chaos at Hickam and Wheeler.

The Army medics took their scissors to Taylor's tux shirt, cutting it off well above the elbow, meanwhile joking about the way the lieutenant was dressed. After they had cleaned the wound with soap and water, the doctor took a look gently squeezing the arm here and there.

"I think, Lieutenant," he said, "the bullet luckily went through your arm between the radius and ulna and missed both. Can't tell 'til we get it x-rayed tomorrow if we can find an x-ray with all the casualties I hear we took all over the island. You have any pain?"

"Not much," replied Taylor. "If you'll bandage it up I'd like to get out of here."

"We'll do that," said the doctor, "and give you some sulfa tablets to stop any infection and APC tablets for pain. Just report to the med unit at Wheeler tomorrow if it hasn't been destroyed, to see if there is any way to get it x-rayed. You think you can fly with it this way?"

"I can fly. No problem with that even if it gets sore overnight."

By the time the medics had bandaged Taylor's arm it was time for the noon meal.

"Let's go get in the chow line," said Welch. "Missed my breakfast and I'm hungry."

By the time the two pilots were outside the medical tent it was nearing 11 a.m. . Taylor pulled Welch aside out of the hearing of anyone around.

"To heck with having chow now, George," whispered Taylor. "Let's get in my car and go try to find some of those Japs we shot down."

Welch already had the keys to the Taylor Buick so they quickly walked to where the car was parked and got in.

As they left the Haleiwa strip, while Welch drove Taylor was looking in the fields on both sides of the road.

"This may be like looking for a needle in a haystack, but I think one of us got a Jap torpedo bomber somewhere around here," said Taylor. "Keep an eye out for the crash site."

Even though Welch was not driving at near the speed he had pushed the Buick on the early morning ride from Wheeler to Haleiwa, it was still leaving a trail of dust behind it heading down the old macadam road.

Suddenly in the distance both pilots could see the "rooster tail" dust trail of an approaching vehicle.

"Who the hell do you think that is?" asked Taylor. "Looks like a convertible."

Within a few minutes the two vehicles had both stopped about fifty feet apart on the narrow road.

The door of the convertible opened and Capt. Austin jumped out, a regulation Colt .45 pistol in his hand aimed at the Buick's occupants.

Taylor was the first out of the Buick.

"Hey, sir," he spoke calmly, "Nice to see you."

Welch also had stepped out of the Buick, not knowing whether to be alarmed or amused at their squadron commander holding them at gunpoint.

"What's going on here?" asked Austin, eyeing Taylor with his tux pants and shirt with one sleeve cut off. "Why are you leaving the field when the Japs have just started a war?"

Taylor looked at Welch, then back to Capt. Austin.

"Sir, Welch and I got up and shot down a few of the Japs," he said. "We thought since the action seems to be over we'd go out and see if we could find some of the planes we downed."

"You shot down some of the Japs?"

Austin holstered his pistol and walked up to shake hands and congratulate his two flight leaders.

"Yessir," said Welch. "We got some bombers over around Ewa, probably headed for Pearl Harbor. Then we rearmed at Wheeler and got a few more here and there."

A big smile came on Austin's face. He had known that behind their goofoff military attitude on the ground, his judgment in naming them as 47th flight leaders had paid off.

"What happened to your arm?" he asked, looking at Taylor.

"Bullet came down through the canopy, hit my trim tab and the doc thinks it went through my arm between the two bones, whatever they're called."

Austin nodded.

"That looks like some wreckage over there," said the squadron commander, pointing to a mass of metal about a hundred yards away on one side of the road. "Let's go see what we've got."

He was a tall man and his two smaller lieutenants had to hustle to keep up with him as he made his way toward the wreckage. When they were there, it was evident it was a torpedo bomber. The pilot and rear gunner both were dead, slumped over in their seats in the wreckage of the fuselage.

"Which one of you got this Jap?" asked Austin.

Both Taylor and Welch shrugged.

"I don't think we know, captain," said Welch. "We were pretty much just focusing on shooting at whatever we saw and saving our own asses. Lot of Jap planes up there today all over the island. I think we were kind of outnumbered."

Austin turned from scanning the wreckage to look at his two pilots.

"I'm damned proud of you guys. Good work. Now let's get on back to the field."

Back at Haleiwa, noon chow was being served so the three of them grabbed mess kits and got in line.

"Sir, where were you this morning?" asked Welch, careful to pose the question in a tone that didn't suggest their leader had shirked his duty by not getting up in one of the squadron planes.

"Well, goddamnit, of all the days that we could have chosen a few of us flew over to Molokai to hunt some deer and look for emergency landing sites. When we got the word the Japs were attacking, we couldn't believe it. And as we came back over Pearl Harbor, our own gunners damned near shot us down. They bombed the hell out of almost everything at Wheeler. Gen. Davidson said they made two attacks about an hour apart. Looks like the planes in our group may be about the only ones left. Gen.

Short's order to group the other Wheeler planes together on the ramp was one helluva great mistake."

"George and I were out a little late and still asleep at Wheeler. By the time we got our clothes on and outside the BOQ, they were blasting the hell out of everything."

Austin again looked down at the tux clothes Taylor was wearing, blood stains on the left leg.

"Yeah," laughed the proud squadron leader, "I can see you got dressed in a hurry."

At that point Lt. Rogers, who had gotten a plane up, joined them.

"How'd you do, Bob?" asked Austin, glad another of his pilots had been able to get up for the action.

"Gordon, by the time I got out here and checked out the situation with our guys and then got my own ship in the air, I didn't have an opportunity to mix it up with the Jap planes. Sorry, but I didn't get close enough to shoot down anything."

The 47th's ground crews in the chow line wore a mixture of overalls wet with sweat and those with white salt stains from dried sweat on their backs and under their arms, and their body odors mixed with the smell of the hot dogs and beans being served for noon chow.

Eating hurriedly, Austin and Rogers headed back to the headquarters tent to await orders on what to do. Based on the vast destruction Austin had seen flying over Pearl Harbor and Wheeler, he doubted the Japs would be back after refueling and rearming on the carriers. After all, there was not much left for targets although he did not know what had happened at Hickham and Bellows fields.

That afternoon when the few 47th planes that got in the air were back at Haleiwa, the only pilot unaccounted for was Lt. John Dains.

The ground crews immediately started refueling and rearming the P-40s and pushing them so they were scattered along the runway and not so close together and vulnerable to bombs as they had been at Wheeler.

From phone calls to operations, Austin learned Haleiwa for whatever reason was the only one of the Army airfields still intact with little harm having been done by the strafing run of a lone Japanese plane.

In the chaos Gen. Short's Army high command and Adm. Kimmel's Navy headquarters were trying to sort out authentic reports of new enemy activity from rumors by the dozens.

At Hickam two or three A-20s and a B-17 had been sent up and directed toward the south to do reconnaissance and see if they could spot the Jap fleet.

At Pearl Harbor the word was the Navy and Marines were still fighting fires and trying to rescue men trapped in the ships. The story was the U.S.S. Arizona had been sunk with one bomb with most of the ship's personnel never able to escape the watery grave.

With the 47th pilots and planes on standby, Austin had resisted orders from operations to get a few planes up to survey the damage for the Army high command.

In one heated conversation with ops in mid-afternoon, Austin said, "Everybody on this island is so trigger-happy I can tell you from what happened to us flying in from Molokai somebody is going to try to shoot down anything they see in the sky. It will be suicide to send my boys up there now, and besides we need every plane and pilot *because we now are the Army Air Corps in Hawaii."*

But just before sundown Gen. Davidson called Austin and told him to get some of his squadron's aircraft up because there was a report Jap planes had been spotted by a ship heading for Oahu.

Captains usually do not argue with generals, so Austin ordered Taylor, Welch and four other planes to go up and see what they could find.

"I don't like this," said Taylor as they rode in the back of a jeep out to where their planes were parked. "We're having a blackout here on the island and the Jap pilots can't see in the dark any better than we can so why the hell would they be coming back now?"

Welch shrugged. He was eager to get back in the air and they would just have to obey orders and take their chances.

All around them the squadron's ground crews in their utility uniforms soaked with sweat and haggard, had weary looks on their faces from a long day of arming, fueling and pushing planes around—dispersing them around in the sand under trees. In between taking care of the planes most had been digging foxholes for some protection. As fast as they dug in the dry sand it would slide back into the bottom of the hole.

And nary a man in the squadron was not marveling at the will of the gods that somehow kept their field safe except from one short burst of fire from a passing Japanese plane early that morning.

After the P-40s were aloft and getting into formation at 10,000 feet, the setting sun reflected off the planes' plexiglas canopies, turning them into an orange color.

"Okay, men," Taylor called on the radio. "We've got to stay over the water and watch for any ships patrolling around so some stupid sonofabitch doesn't start shooting at us."

In the far distance toward Wheeler and Pearl Harbor the pilots could see faint glows of fires still burning there.

And then there was just darkness.

After a few minutes, Welch's voice came over Taylor's radio.

"Where we going, Grits? To China?"

By then Taylor realized that in the near total blackness he had a serious case of vertigo, his P-40 flying in a topsy-turvy world where there was no up or down or right or left.

"Boys," he called to his fellow pilots, "we are going back to Haleiwa or we're going to end up in the damn ocean."

"I can guess the alternative," said Welch, sarcastically, "we get a court martial for disobeying orders."

"Hell," responded Taylor, "they've already got you and me for taking off the second time over at Wheeler, so why not get us another one?"

Back at Haleiwa, the ground crews recognized the sounds of the Allison engines somewhere above them and had enough training to turn on jeep and truck headlights to illuminate the PSP strip for the landing.

Once on the ground the other pilots headed for their tents while Taylor and Welch went to the headquarters.

Inside the tent Austin and Rogers with the corporal at his desk were smoking and waiting for any commands from ops.

The two lieutenants stood at attention until Austin told them to sit.

"Sir," said Taylor, "I had vertigo. There was no way to tell how we were flying up there and to be honest I came down to save our lives instead of crashing into the ocean."

The two commanders were silent, considering the situation the flight had been in trying to stay away from friendly fire. They also were much concerned because they still had no word on what had happened to Dains, hoping that if his ship had been hit he might have parachuted onto land or in the water.

Just then the phone rang and after the corporal answered, he motioned that the call was for Capt. Austin.

Austin went over, took the phone and listened with a surprised look on his face. He said only "Yessir," and hung up.

"That was Gen. Davidson. Bob, he's coming over to pick up these guys so they can tell him what they did today as he continues driving around Wheeler to check on the various situations there."

"Gentlemen," said Rogers, "I suggest you quickly go wash up a little and change into khakis if you have any out here. You won't be doing any more flying tonight."

About twenty minutes later a jeep with four MPs in it and a staff car pulled up in the Haleiwa parking area.

Gen. Davidson walked into the command tent alone and the five men there stood at attention and saluted.

"At ease," said the general, taking a chair at the table and lighting a cigarette. "Gordon, you've had some time now to take stock of the situation. How are we doing?"

"Sir, I'm very proud of the men in the 47th. We can't be certain but it looks like they may have shot down as many as ten of the Japs. But we have one man, Lt. Dains, missing and unaccounted for. We hope maybe he was able to bail out wherever he was and will show up tomorrow."

"That's great," said Gen. Davidson, an officer Austin and Rogers had come to respect during the time they had served with him. "We'll try to get a couple of ships up looking for your missing pilot tomorrow.

"Over at Wheeler, or what's left of it, Sanders, Rasmussen and Brown were able to get planes up and claim they bagged one Jap each. But, it looks like you have most of what's left of airworthy planes right here. Forget the plan to spend this week at strafing practice at Bellows. Bring the squadron back to Wheeler at daybreak tomorrow and make certain they are fully armed and fueled at all times. If the Japs come back, we're damned sure going to be ready for them."

The general stood and his charges jumped to their feet at attention.

"Welch, you and Taylor come with me. I want to hear what you did today directly from you while I make my rounds back at Wheeler. That is if some trigger happy fool doesn't shoot our asses off when we get back there."

Austin, Rogers and the corporal saluted as the general walked out with Taylor and Welch.

At the staff car, Lt. Rasmussen was in the front with the driver so the general told Taylor and Welch to get in the back seat with him and the MP jeep took the lead heading back down the road to Wheeler. Once at the home base, Gen. Davidson told his driver to stop the car at the Officer's Club and drop off Lt. Rasmussen, who during the ride from Wheeler to Haleiwa had told about his dogfight in which he was victorious but came back with a P-36 completely riddled with bullet holes.

Once they had gone through the gate into Wheeler the stench of burning rubber from the tires of the planes on the ramp overwhelmed the smell of their cigarette smoke and fouled the air as they started a tour of the base.

"How's the arm, lieutenant?"

"Sir, the doc fixed it up. Wants me to get it x-rayed tomorrow but there isn't much pain and all I have to watch for is an infection."

"Welch, how many Japs do you think you bagged today?"

"Sir, it was crazy up there but I know four I hit were headed down and I think maybe two more fell somewhere but I can't swear to it."

"Taylor, how about you?"

"Well, after we left Haleiwa we got back to Wheeler real fast and all the Japs were gone. Next thing we ran into the B-17s and then we spotted the line of bombers about over Ewa, so we started picking them off from the end of the line. I got one for sure and I think maybe a couple went down in the water. But like Lt. Welch just said, it was really crazy up there. But the bombers were no match for the P-40 and somehow we were able to get the rear gunners every time."

"Were both of you at Haleiwa this morning? How did you first know about the other bases being attacked? I know you were not on duty for the weekend. Did ops call and alert you that Wheeler was being attacked?"

"Uh, oh no sir," said Welch. "Lt. Taylor and I had been out partying last night so we sacked out in our quarters at Wheeler. Loud noise woke us up about 0800 and we both got dressed and ran outside to see what was going on. When we saw it was Japs, we took off for Haleiwa in Taylor's car."

"Now, let me get this straight," said the general, blowing cigarette smoke out the right rear window where by protocol the senior officer had the right rear seat.

"On your own you drove out to Haleiwa, got in your planes and started looking for the action without any orders from anyone?"

"Well," said Welch, somewhat hesitantly. "Lt. Rogers got there about the same time Lt. Taylor and I arrived, but I think he was trying to get things organized for whenever the Japs attacked Haleiwa. The ground crew had two planes all ready for us so we just got in and took off."

"All on your own?"

"Yessir," both Taylor and Welch answered simultaneously.

"Then, you ran out of ammo over at Ewa and landed at Wheeler to get some fifties. And after I came out there and my staff guys got up on your wings telling you to disperse your ships and not go up again, you disobeyed my orders and went up for a second time."

That was a moment of truth for the two lieutenants. Each waited for the other to speak with neither knowing what to say. After a few moments of silence Taylor spoke.

"Sir, I can only speak for myself and not Lt. Welch. When I was in training to get my wings and commission and then in the seven or eight months I've been out here with the 47th, it's been all about protecting my country from its enemies.

"I don't know what has been happening back in Washington but as of about 0300 hours when I went to sleep we were not in a war with Japan. But when I woke up Lt. Welch and I could see we were being attacked by Japs. So I think what happened was that when we saw the second bunch of Japs heading in to attack Wheeler again, my training just automatically kicked in and I felt it was my duty to do what I could to go up and shoot down those sonofabitches. Under the circumstances the thought never entered my head I was disobeying your orders."

"Sir," said Welch," that's exactly the way I felt. I meant no disrespect, sir, I just instinctively wanted to fight as I've been trained to do."

Gen. Davidson laughed as he stubbed his cigarette out in the little ashtray on the inside of the door that already was full of butts.

"Well, gentlemen, here is the deal. Maybe what we had there was a failure to communicate with what my aides told you. By the time you landed, we knew there was no small number of attackers. Having no idea the Japs would make a second run on Wheeler, I had serious doubts about sending two of my best pilots to go up against such overwhelming odds.

"You were very heroic in my opinion go up a second time and luckily you survived it. You were right in what you did and I was wrong. So let me get this straight. In terms of disobeying my order, you are absolved. On the first flight you didn't know the size of the Jap task force. When you went up again you did know. To tell you the truth, you don't know how much I envy what you did today and I only wish I was still a second lieutenant and could have done the same thing."

Taylor and Welch both were much relieved.

"Thank you, sir," said Taylor.

"Yessir, we appreciate that," said Welch.

Even in the few hours since they had landed at Haleiwa, both had expected they would be slapped with a court martial for disobeying the general's order to not go up again. Both had imagined being busted down to enlisted men and turned into mechanics or desk jockeys.

Gen. Davidson with the MP jeep leading the way took a tour around the perimeter of Wheeler, stopping here and there to chat with his men on duty at the antiaircraft and machine gun emplacements.

The MP's jeep had a small red light blinking on it and they approached all the troops with extreme caution, hearing some small arms fire during one or two of the stops. All the troops were surprised to see the general and were obviously edgy not knowing what to expect.

One of the main hits by the Japanese had been the ammo storage area at Wheeler where, by orders of Gen. Short, all the antiaircraft shells and other bullets not being used by the troops on Alert One for sabotage guarding planes and other key facilities were kept. It had taken most of the afternoon to rearm weapons with the ammo salvaged from the bomb hit.

Even by the faint light from the jeep and staff car Taylor and Welch were stunned by the damage at Wheeler. Bulldozers had been ordered to push the wreckage of the base's airplanes that had been on the ramp into small hills. In one pile a P-40 wing was sticking into the air with its white star with the red center on a blue field highlighting the destruction.

Some hangars were no more than steel skeletons after having been burned and some buildings were just heaps of ashes on the ground.

"I had another piece of good luck besides that round hitting my cockpit," Taylor told the general. "When I ran to the lanai at my BOQ to call Haleiwa, one of the Jap planes sent a row of bullets right down the hallway beside where I was standing."

Gen. Davidson laughed.

"You think two pieces of luck? How you and Lt. Welch stayed in the air that long without being shot down says a lot both about your flying skill *and your luck*. I don't imagine any of the Jap pilots who came over here today were just out of flight school."

The general said that afternoon he had toured Hickam with Gen. Martin, who was suffering from an ulcer and probably should have been in a hospital, and the devastation down there had been almost unimaginable.

"We lost hundreds of good Army men on the island today," the general spoke with melancholy in his voice. "I talked with a Sgt. Turley from your squadron who said he was in the mess hall eating breakfast, and ran out to see arms and legs and other body parts scattered all around. Apparently he got in one of those ditches they dug out to the tents with another man when they were strafing the hell out of that area."

He said the devastation at Hickam was especially heartbreaking.

When Hickam was on Ford Island in the middle of Pearl Harbor and eventually run off by the Navy, it had grabbed a large piece of real estate nearby that had been expanded to be an enormous base with state-of-the-art facilities—especially its Officers' Club with a bar, dining room and exercise facility. It was named for the late Lt. Col. Horace Meek Hickam, who had been killed February, 1934 in a plane crash at Fort Crockett near Galveston. At the club white dress uniforms or black tie were standard every night.

When deciding how to build the barracks at what would be called "bomberland," the official who wanted to build a huge facility that would house all troops won out over another who preferred smaller units scattered around the base.

The result was a monstrous barracks built next to the hangars housing 3,200 men and was in fact a city with barbershops, laundry, dispensary, post exchange and numerous other facilities.

And, Gen. Davidson related to his young pilots that the Japanese had bombed and strafed the hell out of the barracks and most other facilities at the base.

"It now bears no resemblance to what it was at daybreak today," Gen. Davidson said.

For Taylor and Welch, their own elation at having gotten into the air and scored some kills had no meaning at all as they saw the damage at Wheeler and heard what had happened at the other Army bases.

The general explained they had not yet figured out from which direction the attackers came, and with so many of the long-range aircraft destroyed the question was which way to send them to look for the enemy fleet.

"We had our boys that could get up after the attack yesterday scouting out to the south and they found nothing," the general said. "Come daylight we'll be trying again."

It would be some time before the Army and Navy learned Adm. Yamamoto had sent his planes in from the north.

Around midnight, Gen. Davidson arranged for a jeep to take Taylor and Welch back to Haleiwa.

"You've made me very proud," said the general as he said good night to the two pilots. "I'm going over to Fort Shafter and Tripler to see how my wounded troops are doing and I'm sure I'll be seeing you tomorrow."

After being driven back to Haleiwa, Taylor and Welch lit cigarettes and looked up at a clear sky with twinkling stars. Right then, their so-called great luck in being assigned to Hawaii did not exactly seem as if they had been seen sent to duty in "paradise."

"Funny," said Welch, "we've been talking for months about places where we might be sent such as to England or the Philippines to fight in a war, and I'll be damned if the war doesn't come right to us here in Hawaii."

"Well," mused Taylor, "at least one major situation has happened to us today. Now we both know how we we'll act when we get up there to mix it up with the other guys. My only regret is that you got that bastard who shot me because I sure wanted to nail his ass myself."

They both laughed, stomped out their cigarettes and headed for their tents. It had been far and away the longest and most interesting day of their young lives.

Current events of that day: The Japanese pulled a surprise attack on most of the military facilities on the Island of Oahu, Territory of Hawaii. All liquor stores in Honolulu were closed until further notice. Hickam Field issued a call for drinking water. A Japanese aircraft carrier was reported sunk off Hawaii (This did not happen.). The U.S. Coast Guard was told to grab Finnish ships. Navy To Shoot at All Ships Not Identified (headlines). Ensign John F. Kennedy, a future war hero and president of the United States, attended a professional football game in Washington, DC. where the Redskins defeated Philadelphia 20–14.

Epilogue

"The first casualty of war is the truth."
—Rep. Tom Davis (R-VA) at the House
Committee on Oversight and Government
Reform Hearing on "Misleading
Information from the Battlefield,"
April 24, 2007, Washington, DC.

The dawning of Dec. 8, 1941 in Hawaii probably was the most ambiguous greeting of a sunrise in the history of the military since Francis Scott Key in 1814 waited to see if "The Star Spangled Banner" would still be waving that morning over Fort McHenry.

Chaos had reigned the night before throughout the island in deep shock and reeling from the Sunday morning surprise attack by Adm. Yamamoto's estimated 350 aircraft.

Rumors of another attack and/or an invasion spread throughout Oahu after the Japanese pilots had headed back to their carriers before noon.

In the darkness of Sunday night weapons were fired at imagined Japanese soldiers, American troops were killed by friendly fire and there could have been little peaceful sleep either by the military or civilians.

Dawn on Monday brought to the military the realization that what had happened the day before was not just a terrible nightmare, but also a disaster of indescribable scope and magnitude.

For the top Army and Navy commanders in Hawaii, communicating the damage inflicted on their facilities to the military bosses in Washington, DC was no less than signing death warrants for their own careers.

Amid the Pearl Harbor devastation sailors, marines and civilians worked throughout the night to rescue those trapped beneath the water in ships, as engineers and other planners looked at what must be done to salvage some of the badly damaged fleet.

The major disaster by far at Pearl was the sinking of the U.S.S. Arizona by one Japanese bomb. It sat on the bottom of the harbor with most of its crew, 1177 men, lost forever.

The U.S.S. Oklahoma had capsized and the six other battleships were damaged in varying degrees along with most other vessels anchored in the harbor.

Ens. Charles Barry, who was assigned to the U.S.S. Blue, a destroyer, had weekend liberty and was staying on Waikiki at the Ala Moana Hotel where his skipper and wife also were guests.

Barry and his skipper had a Sunday morning tennis date but when he called his superior's room, he was told by the wife that Pearl was under attack and her husband had left for the Blue.

Barry grabbed his gear and ran down to the street. The only vehicle around was a Army jeep with a driver waiting for a colonel, also at the hotel.

"The Japs are attacking and we are going to Pearl Harbor, and that's an order," the young ensign told the driver and off they went.

When Barry arrived at the dock, the Blue had been one of the first ships to get underway with four ensigns having taken command before the skipper arrived. The U.S.S. Detroit, a cruiser, was about to leave its docking space so Barry got aboard.

The Blue did well under the young officers patrolling the waters around Pearl Harbor after the attack but was sunk Aug. 23, 1942 at Guadalcanal. The Detroit was at sea for a week before returning to Pearl. In the meantime, Barry's parents received a Red Cross telegram notifying them their son was missing in action since no one at Pearl knew he was on another ship.

At the Army airfields the remainder of the daylight hours Sunday had been used to get treatment for the wounded, the dead moved into makeshift morgues, destroyed and damaged aircraft pushed off ramps and inventories taken at the various bases as to what remained that could be counted on to repel any new attacks.

Some of the few aircraft still intact, A-20s and B-17s, on Sunday afternoon had been sent out on patrol to try to locate Adm. Yamamoto's task force and found nothing by flying in the opposite direction.

What was remaining for mounting a defense among the Army facilities could be summed up in two words: damned little.

Had the Japanese returned for another attack on Monday, there would not have been much more left of the Army Air Corps than the two dozen planes of the 47th squadron and a few others that survived the bombing and strafing at Hickam and Wheeler fields. Against Yamamoto's more than 300 aircraft back on his carriers, aerial combat would have been short lived against such overwhelming odds.

Early in the day Monday news came from Washington that Congress, at President Roosevelt's request in a brief but eloquent speech before a Joint Session, had declared war on Japan and there was no doubt but that a state of war also now existed with the Axis powers in Europe although it was not formally declared by the U.S. until Dec. 11.

In Roosevelt's speech he was careful to ask that the declaration of war against Japan be retroactive to Sunday, December 7 so it could not be said that American forces attacked those of another country while not in a state of war.

By midafternoon on the day of the attack, one would think both Adm. Kimmel and Gen. Short surely knew, as assessments of the damage at Pearl and the various Army bases came in, their careers were finished. They also must have known they would not for long command forces in a war the United States by default had just entered.

(One author has written that Adm. Kimmel did not really understand until three days later that his Navy career was finished. This may be true, but how does one rise to the rank of admiral in the Navy and not know immediately that "the old man" always is responsible when things go wrong?)

The next morning, Monday, Dec. 8, Capt. Austin led the 47th Squadron back to Wheeler which at least gave the base an additional two dozen usable aircraft. Still missing was 2nd Lt. John Dains. It later would be confirmed he was shot down by friendly fire as was the situation for several Navy aircraft flying in to Ford Island from the carrier Enterprise.

Meanwhile efforts began almost immediately to restore the damaged hangars, barracks and other facilities at Wheeler, Hickham and Bellows fields and Schofield Barracks.

The decision was made at Wheeler to restore hangars and the operations building to the original structures before the attack and there they stand today amid the great, grassy field.

With none of the Navy carriers having been anchored in Pearl during the attack, they brought in more P-40s to replace those destroyed at the Army bases or shot down.

As with virtually all statistics in various books and documentaries about what happened on December 7, 1941, the numbers of Army planes destroyed varies from fifty to ninety-five percent.

The data on those killed and wounded, aircraft destroyed and damaged and other statistics are maddening for an author to deal with doing research with what hopefully would be reliable sources.

Here are some examples from several sources about the most important statistic, number of deaths, resulting from the attack on the Army bases.

The Pearl Harbor Fiftieth Anniversary Fact Sheet lists 218 Army deaths.

Ernest Arroyo's "Pearl Harbor" lists 233 Army dead.

The Pearl Harbor History Associates also list 233 Army deaths.

"7 December 7 1941 The Air Force Story," an official Air Force book published in 2001, the 60th anniversary of Pearl Harbor, lists by name and serial number 233 Army personnel killed in action, 33 more men than was in the 47th Squadron back then, and 439 wounded.

And that is the point of this book, "the *other* Pearl Harbor."

What happened to the Army personnel and its facilities has largely been ignored by historians and the media as well as erroneous reporting in what little has been written and said about this branch of the services.

An exception is "7 December 1941 The Air Force Story," while published fifty years after the event at least tries to make the case that the Army also was deeply involved in the first battle of World War II by virtue of Congress having made the declaration of war retroactive to the attack on Hawaii.

In books and documentaries, for example, there also are all sorts of numbers for the total fleet of Japanese planes in the attack.

Even in the Air Force history, on one page it gives a total number for the Japanese planes attacking Hawaii and on another page, listing these aircraft by the various types of fighters and bombers, they do not add up to the same total.

Contradictions abound and seventy years later there is no way, no matter how much a particular part of the attack is researched, an author can state without the possibility of contradiction precisely what happened. But this writing reflects nine years trying.

Gordon W. Prange, Donald M. Goldstein and Katherine V. Dillon are among the most noted of all those who have written about the Pearl Harbor attack. Yet in one of their books they write about gawkers at Schofield Barracks watching Lt. Rasmussen's P-36 in a prolonged dogfight with a Japanese plane. On another page they describe the vicious attacks by the Japanese on Schofield facilities as being near total chaos.

It begs the question, with Japanese planes bombing and strafing Schofield were there really people standing around watching a dogfight? Apparently they were.

A woman working for a Hawaii tourism company with a desk in the lobby of a Waikiki hotel in May, 2007 said she as a youngster, with her hair in a pigtail, was being taken somewhere on Schofield by her nanny. As they left the house, her mother heard the planes and ran out to grab her daughter by the pigtail and pull her back. The nanny, she said, was killed from the strafing by a Japanese plane.

In the 2001 interview Gen. Taylor is very specific in his story that he and Welch drove at top speed for Haleiwa only minutes after the Japanese attacked Wheeler, got in their P-40s and flew over to attack a string of Japanese bombers near the Marine base at Ewa, shot down some planes and then landed at Wheeler Field to rearm.

After being told by "the brass," as he always described those officers who jumped up on his plane and Welch's at Wheeler and ordered them not to take off again, Gen. Taylor said he and Welch did anyway just as the second wave of Japanese planes approached Wheeler. Out of ammo again, Gen. Taylor said, they landed back at Haleiwa to get his car and go look for some of the planes they shot down that morning.

Maj. Gen. Austin USAF Ret., their squadron commander at the time, in two lengthy interviews and numerous phone conversations in recent years has confirmed Gen. Taylor's 2001 version. So have other members of the 47th Squadron contacted over the years.

In the Roberts Commission testimony (later in the Epilogue) Lts. Taylor and Welch related somewhat different and very much confusing details about what happened that day.

As Lt Taylor said in his testimony, "… it is kind of jumbled in my mind … "

This is very understandable, considering the young age of the two second lieutenants and, as fairly new pilots with no experience in real aerial combat, having been up against such enormous odds that day.

Ironically, it was the Army–perhaps because it's Air Corps' mission was to protect Pearl Harbor—that first moved to put its public relations operation into high gear early in the week after the attack. Or to create major "spin" as it is now called.

It is difficult to imagine that with the hundreds of deaths, destruction and vast number of wounded personnel, the Army high command could come up with a brilliant public relations plan to divert attention from its not having been better prepared.

The Army plan was simple. Have the War Department in Washington, DC quickly announce that Lts. Taylor and Welch would be the first two designated heroes of World War II and both would be awarded the Distinguished Service Cross.

The DSC is not the Army's garden variety medal for heroism. And it can only be awarded for heroism in combat whereas the Medal of Honor numerous times has been bestowed on those, such as Charles Lindbergh after his historic flight to Paris, for peacetime achievements.

The DSC ranks just below the Congressional Medal of Honor and normally is awarded only after considerable research and statements by those who witnessed the heroic action.

But with the approval of Gen. George C. Marshall, head of the U.S. War Department, Communiqué No. 19 (a fancy name for a press release) was issued only six days after the Pearl Harbor attack on Dec. 13 naming Taylor and Welch for these honors.

The Washington bureau of United Press (later UPI) picked up on the release that Saturday afternoon and put a story on its wire that stated in part:

"The Distinguished Service Cross—highest honor the Army can bestow—was awarded tonight to two brave young fliers for 'extraordinary heroism in action' during Japan's surprise dawn attack against Hawaii December 7.

"Honored were 2nd Lieutenants George S. Welch, 23, of Wilmington, Del., and Kenneth M. Taylor, 22, of Hominy, Okla., who, between them, shot down six enemy planes in savage aerial fighting over the Island of Oahu.

"They became the first men so honored in World War II. The decorations were announced in Army Communiqué No. 19 which said:

"'These awards are the first of a number to be given for heroism in Hawaii and the Philippines during the present conflict. The others will be made in the future.'"

It was a masterful stroke on the part of the Army. The story ran in virtually every daily newspaper in America for the Sunday, Dec. 14 issues.

Days later the recently promoted Maj. Austin was ordered to arrange the medal ceremony for his two pilots on Jan. 8, 1942 at Wheeler Field, with all available personnel turned out in the old "wash pan" helmets, side arms and gas masks.

The movie newsreel companies such as Universal and Fox produced footage of the medal ceremony, which was featured in theaters coast to coast. By any criteria, awarding of the medals was a great public relations success.

Taylor and Welch, according to Gen. Austin, their former squadron leader, were whisked back to the mainland for a public relations tour and the positive publicity about the two young heroes continued for months.

But in a large scrapbook kept by Taylor's mother and filled with newspaper and other memorabilia of her son's early Air Corps career, there is not a single clip or other evidence of this tour.

Welch, the senior of the two and awarded his medal first, in May, 1942 made a "support the war" tour back on the mainland and was congratulated by President Roosevelt on May 25 at the White House.

In the July 13, 1942 issue of Life Magazine Lt. Welch is pictured in Hollywood at the end of his publicity tour with Betty Garble, Claudette Colbert and other major female stars.

But almost as quickly as the Army had produced two new heroes, President Franklin D. Roosevelt on Dec. 18, 1941 moved to name a commission to investigate the attack.

With Americans eager for any good news as the country tooled up for another world war, the heroism of the two pilots and their comrades overshadowed this appointment—the first of nine investigations into how our military leaders in Hawaii could have been blindsided when the nation was so close to a war with Japan.

The first investigation was called the Roberts Commission, and it's work was not so prolonged as the Warren Commission on President Kennedy's assassination or the 9/11 Commission on the Sept. 11, 2001 terrorist attacks, lasting only from Dec. 18, 1941 to Jan. 23, 1942.

The Commission was named after Owen J. Roberts, an associate justice of the U.S. Supreme Court. The chair for the Congressional investigators was U. S. Sen. Alben W. Barkley (D-KY), later vice president under President Harry Truman.

Both Lts. Taylor and Welch were called to testify before the Roberts Commission.

It could be deduced from their testimony that the two pilots who had not been intimidated by 350 Japanese planes on Dec. 7 were scared out of their khaki pants appearing before Sen. Barkley and the Commission's high-ranking military interrogators.

Sen. Barkley asked a few questions but most came from the military experts including Gen. Frank R. McCoy, Gen. Joseph T. McNarney and Adm. W.H. Standley, a former chief of naval operations.

Writing seventy years later with the blinding clarity of hindsight, to the author many of the questions were just simply inane and it was not until near the end of the testimony that the military brass got to the point: was there a workable, practiced plan in place for the defense against an aerial attack against the military facilities on Hawaii on Dec. 7, 1941?

From the transcript of their testimony before the Joint Committee on the Investigation of the Pearl Harbor Attack (Roberts Commission), here are selected questions and answers:

Lt. Taylor's testimony (in part):

"General McCoy. We would like to have a narrative from you first. Give whatever information you know and simply tell us what happened to you during the morning of the attack until your own activities were over that day. Just give us a running narrative without any attempt to give us more than just what happened, what you saw and what you did.

"Lieutenant Taylor. Well, sir, on the morning of the 7th I was at Wheeler Field at the Officers' Club when the bombing began. Lieutenant Welch and I got in my car and drove to Haleiwa. We had been in the field there for the past week or thereabouts, as one squadron is at all times recently.

"When we got out there mostly new men were there. I saw the new men, and so Lieutenant Welch and I took two planes that they were servicing and got ready to go up. We had called them or somebody had called them; so they were practically ready when we arrived.

"There were some other officers there getting ready to take off, but I think they followed us in about thirty minutes; I am not sure, but Lieutenant Welsh (sic) and myself started patrolling the island. There wasn't any .50 caliber ammunition, so we landed at the field. That was between the first bombing and the second bombing. I got .50 caliber ammunition in my plane and Lieutenant Welsh got some in his.

"From there on things got kind of jumbled, because we took off, and as we took off they were coming over the field.

"The Chairman. This is the second attack?

"Lieutenant Taylor. Yes. We landed three times, it seems like. It is kind of jumbled in my mind which time we did go back, but I would say this time they were going very low over Pearl Harbor, and the men left, and I took my plane around and took off right into them so they could not run me down too easy. I made a nice turn out into them and got in the string of six or eight planes. I don't know how many there were. I was in them. I was on one's tail as we went over Waialua, firing at the one next to me, and there was one following firing at me, and I pulled out. I don't know what happened to the other plane. Lieutenant Welch, I think, shot the other man down. Then we patrolled some more over Ewa. At that time there was a whole string of planes looking like a traffic pattern. We went down and got in the traffic pattern and shot down several planes there. I know for certain I had shot down two planes or perhaps more; I don't know.

"At that time Lieutenant Welsh and I got separated. He came back to Wheeler Field but I believe I landed about three times. I just landed and got ammunition and went back. I think that is all.

"The Chairman. Were you getting breakfast at the time of the attack?

"Lieutenant Taylor. No, sir, I was still in bed when the first bomb hit. I thought a Navy man had probably gone off the main route, so I didn't get up until the second one and then went out just as they were machine-gunning the club at that time, and they were machine-gunning all around while we were driving for the post."

And, then:

"General McNarney. Who is your squadron commander?

"Lieutenant Taylor. Major Austin.

"General McNarney. Where was he?

"Lieutenant Taylor. He was on Molokai.

"The Chairman. He had been sent there on some special mission?

"Lieutenant Taylor. No, sir, he was deer hunting over the weekend.

"The Chairman. He was on leave?

"Lieutenant Taylor. Yes.

"General McNarney. Who was in charge of the squadron?

"Lieutenant Taylor. Lieutenant Rogers.

"General McNarney. Where was he?

"Lieutenant Taylor. He was there when I got there at the field. He was at the field at the time and later took up a plane.

"General McNarney. You say you and Lieutenant Welch went and took off.

"Lieutenant Taylor. Yes.

"General McNarney. Were you directed to go up by anybody or did you just go on your own initiative?

"Lieutenant Taylor. No, sir.

"General McNarney. You were not directed by anyone?

"Lieutenant Taylor. No, sir. We were not directed by anybody. He (Welch) was the assistant operations officer so we just went up.

"General McNarney. In other words, no squadron commander gave you any orders? You just took off on your own initiative?

"Lieutenant Taylor. No, sir, there was nobody there who could give us orders with the exception of Lieutenant Rogers, so we went ahead and took off. I imagine the orders would be the same."

Finally:

"General McCoy. Do I understand that you have received a commendation from the Department since the attack?

"Lieutenant Taylor. Yes, sir.

"General McCoy. In what form?

"Lieutenant Taylor. I understand I am to receive the D.S.C. All I know is just what I read in the newspapers.

"General McCoy. I congratulate you.

"Lieutenant Taylor. Thank you, sir.

"The Chairman. Thank you, sir. We have been glad to have you, lieutenant.

"Lieutenant Taylor. Thank you, sir."

Lt. Welch's testimony (in part):

"General McNarney. Were any of your personnel on the alert or in a state of readiness on December 7?

"Lieutenant Welsh. No, sir.

"General McNarney. Will you tell the Commission what you did personally from the time you heard the first bomb drop?

"Lieutenant Welsh. When I heard them I stayed in the club and then watched for about five or ten minutes, I imagine, and then we got in Lieutenant Taylor's car and drove to Haleiwa.

"General McNarney. What was the condition of the field when you arrived there and what happened?

"Lieutenant Welsh. They had been alterted (sic), apparently, from Wheeler Field, because they were loading the airplanes, and we received orders from control to take off and to proceed to Easy, which was Barber's Point, at 8000 feet.

"General McNarney: How did you get the order from the control? By telephone?

"Lieutenant Welsh: When we got the order, yes. We got over to Easy and did not see any planes. We did not get a radio, so we went around by Wheeler and saw a B-17 and saw Japanese strung out strafing Ewa. I came back to Wheeler Field and the Japs were attacking and came back to Wheeler Field, so we came back to the field and then took off again.

"General McNarney: When you first landed at the field, what was happening at that time?

"Lieutenant Welsh. They were dispersing the airplanes. I got ammunition and gasoline and we took off again.

"General McNarney. Was there any difficulty in getting the ammunition or gasoline?

"Lieutenant Welsh. We had to argue with some of the ground crew. They wanted us to disperse the airplanes and we wanted to fight. Finally I got the ammunition, and just as they were loading some .50 caliber, the Japs came back again. We took off directly into them and shot down some. I shot down one right on Lieutenant Taylor's tail.

"I went back to Ewa and found some more over Barber's Point and engaged them there. Then I came back to Wheeler. I landed there and then I went up and found none around five miles Barber's Point. I continued around for forty-five minutes. I did not have a regular patrol. Then there was no more action.

"General McNarney. How many planes in your squadron did you get in the air?

"Lieutenant Welsh. While the Japs were still over the Island?

"General McNarney. I mean the morning of the attack or during the course of the attack.

"Lieutenant Welsh. I would say four, or maybe six, airplanes. I am sure it was four."

"General McNarney. Who is your squadron commander?

"Lieutenant Welsh. Major Austin.

"General McNarney. Where was he at the time?

"Lieutenant Welsh. He was on the Island of Molokai.

"General McNarney. Who was acting squadron commander?

"Lieutenant Welsh. Lieutenant Rogers is acting squadron commander.

"General McNarney. Where was he?

"Lieutenant Welch. At Wheeler Field.

"The Chairman. Had he been in the Officer's Club there?

"Lieutenant Welsh. No, sir, he was in his own quarters.

"General McNarney. Do you know when he arrived at Haleiwa?

"Lieutenant Welsh. He arrived there about the same time I did. I saw him getting out of his car.

"General McNarney. Did he take off?

"Lieutenant Welsh. He took off, too, about a half hour later, I believe."

And these questions about Welch's social life were really getting to the heart of the matter:

"The Chairman. Where were you on the night of December 6, Saturday night?

"Lieutenant Welsh. At Honolulu, Hickam Field, and Pearl Harbor.

"The Chairman. Did you have a party?

"Lieutenant Welsh. Yes, sir.

"The Chairman. You were on leave?

"Lieutenant Welsh. Yes."

Finally, to a little substance:

"The Chairman. How many planes do you think you got?

"Lieutenant Welsh. I only saw four hits, sir.

"General McCoy. You were given credit for bringing down four planes, were you not?

"Lieutenant Welsh. Yes, sir. I was given credit for five but I did not see the other one.

"The Chairman. Anything further?

"General McCoy. No, sir.

"Admiral Standley. You were assigned to special detail at Haleiwa?

"Lieutenant Welsh. I had a regular duty, yes.

"Admiral Standley. Did you have a tour of duty at Haleiwa with officers assigned to the tour of duty, daytime?

"Lieutenant Welsh. No, sir, our whole squadron was moved to Haleiwa for fifteen days approximately for training in the field.

'Admiral Standley. Your planes were parked there?

"Lieutenant Welsh. Yes, sir.

"Admiral Standley. What sort of guard was over your planes at that time?

"Lieutenant Welsh. I imagine a regular field guard. I am not positive about it, but at least one man for every plane, armed with pistol and rifle.

"Admiral Standley. Were there any officers assigned to duty with that detail so that there was some officer there every day?

"Lieutenant Welsh. Yes, we had an officer there and four or five other, pilots, but they were new pilots and apparently they had never flown P-40s, and we did not take them.

"Admiral Standley. Well, did you at any time stand a tour of duty?

"Lieutenant Welsh. Yes.

"Admiral Standley. During your tour of duty, what was your responsibility as to these planes?

"Lieutenant Welsh. To guard the planes from sabotage. We were on alert for sabotage then. We did not have any instructions against aerial attack; it was all ground defense, and I was to inspect the guard twice during each relief.

"Admiral Standley. How many guards did you have stationed?

"Lieutenant Welsh. At Haleiwa?

"Admiral Standley. Yes.

"Lieutenant Welsh. Twenty-three, sir.

"Admiral Standley. Were they armed?

"Lieutenant Welsh. Yes, with a pistol, and some with pistol and rifle.

"Admiral Standley. Were there any machine guns?

"Lieutenant Welsh. No, sir.

"Admiral Standley. Did they have ammunition?

"Lieutenant Welsh. They had .30 caliber ammunition but no .50 caliber.

"General McCoy: Was there any installation of anti-aircraft guns ready for action then?

"Lieutenant Welsh. No, sir, there were none ready. There were pits dug, but no guns in them.

"Admiral Standley: Were there any instructions issued to those guards as to what to do in case of an enemy airplane coming over?

"Lieutenant Welsh: No, sir.

"Admiral Standley. There was no indication that sabotage might take the nature of an attack from above?

"Lieutenant Welsh. No, sir.

"Admiral Standley. That is all.

"The Chairman. We will ask you not to discuss the testimony that you have given here or anything that has happened in this room?

"General McCoy. I congratulate you on your D.S.C., Lieutenant.

"Lieutenant Welsh. Thank you, sir."

(Author's note: In the testimony Lts. Taylor and Welch refer to their squadron leader as "Maj. Austin." At the time of the attack, Capt. Austin had been promoted to the rank of major but he has said it had not yet become official but was shortly afterwards. While Gordon Austin went on to fight in North Africa and retired as a major general of the U.S. Air Force, it is the author's impression his decision to go to Molokai that weekend is one of the greatest regrets of this old warrior's life. Also, in the testimony transcript George Welch's name is always incorrectly spelled "Welsh.')

It is abundantly clear both Taylor and Welch were not giving an accurate description of what happened that day. For example, there is no evidence anywhere that they went up for a third time, especially since Taylor was injured on the second flight.

Then there is the inconsistency between Gen. Taylor's interview in 2001 about getting the .50 caliber ammo during the reaming at Wheeler for the second flight. Pvt. Sweeney has said Taylor's P-40 had not been synched for the .50 caliber rounds so he was rearmed with .30. Whether Welch had been rearmed with .50s will never be known but most likely his P-40 also had not been synched if Taylor's had not.

If there is a certain "déjà vu" ring to the story of the War Department putting forth two heroes with a full court press by its public relations operation immediately after Pearl Harbor, then think Pvt. Jessica Lynch and Cpl. Pat Tillman and the Pentagon's adulation over these two "heroes" coincidental with the negative stories breaking about the Abu Gharib prison scandal.

Except in the case of Pvt. Lynch and Cpl. Tillman there was no heroism other than that they were in uniform in combat zones.

The Lynch/Tillman cases in time during the Iraq/Afghanistan wars became a major expose when it was revealed the Pentagon had served up to the world two of the biggest canards and most shameful acts by a U.S. government public affairs operation in modern military history.

By the time it was discovered that neither Pvt. Lynch in Iraq nor Cpl. Tillman in Afghanistan had done anything heroic, the Pentagon's publicity blitz had been so successful that even today millions likely do not know the truth.

The true story of the two "heroes" eventually came out.

On April 24, 2007, the U.S. House of Representatives Committee on Oversight and Government Reform held a hearing at the Capitol on "Misleading Information from the Battlefield."

Pvt. Lynch had been portrayed by Army public affairs as having bravely fought, after being injured in a vehicle accident during the invasion of Iraq, until the ammunition in her weapon was expended.

Later, she told U.S. News & World Report testifying before the committee was the "scariest" thing she ever did. Judging from the confusing Taylor/Welch testimony before the Roberts Commission, they must have felt much the same.

She stated at the hearing that she was disoriented by her injuries after the Army vehicle in which she was riding overturned, and never fired a shot.

Pvt. Lynch testified:

"At the same time, tales of great heroism were being told. At my parents' home in Wirt County, West Virginia, it was under siege by media all repeating the story of the 'little girl Rambo' from the hills of West Virginia who went down fighting.' It was not true."

The other "hero" discussed at the hearing was Cpl. Pat Tillman, the former NFL Arizona Cardinals safety who had been hailed as a hero for action in Afghanistan and awarded a Silver Star posthumously.

Some weeks went by before it was revealed Tillman had been killed by friendly fire while trying to signal to his fellow Rangers that he was one of them.

His brother Kevin, also a Ranger serving with Pat in Afghanistan, testified at the House hearing:

"This freshly manufactured narrative was then distributed to the American public and we believe the strategy had the intended effect. It shifted the focus from the grotesque torture at Abu Gharib in a downward spiral of an illegal act of aggression to a great American who died a hero's death."

Later, Kevin Tillman also stated at the hearing:

"Writing a Silver Star award before a single eye-witness account is taken is not a misstep. Falsifying soldier witness statements for a Silver Star is not a misstep. These are intentional falsehoods that meet the legal definition for fraud."

No one questions the Taylor/Welch heroism, only the comparison of how quickly the Pearl Harbor heroes were produced when the Army was under siege for not being prepared on Dec. 7, 1941 as Pvt. Lynch and Cpl. Tillman were designated heroes as the Abu Gharib prison scandal was unfolding.

The obviously rushed announcement of the Taylor/Welch heroism strongly suggests Gen. Walter Short, the top Army commander in Hawaii, was quite naturally trying to provide the country some positive spin to counter the public's shock with what had happened under his command.

But, there are so many flaws in how the Army went about putting forth Taylor and Welch as great heroes amidst the almost total chaos of that week, it raises many questions—not about their heroism, but in the haste with which it was done.

Years of research concerning the hasty awarding of the medals to Taylor and Welch were devoted to finding the "traffic" (military term for communications) between Gen. Short's high command in Hawaii and Gen. George C. Marshall's War Department in Washington.

This was done because the traffic is a requirement by the Army Medals Board for considering upgrades to the

Medal of Honor for Taylor and Welch. This long effort has not been carried on solely by the author, but also by U.S. Sen. Tom Carper (D-DE) and others loyal to George Welch in his home state of Delaware and elsewhere.

When the author's search led to the Air Force Historical Agency at Maxwell AFB in Alabama, eventually a communication was sent to him stating that the traffic regarding the Taylor/Welch medals would be found at the Pentagon.

This seemed unlikely because in years of research on the Taylor/Welch action at Pearl Harbor there had never been any indication any records on them were archived at the Pentagon.

Taylor having been a native of Oklahoma, U.S. Sen. James Inhofe (R-OK), a high-ranking member of he Senate Armed Services Committee, was asked to assist in locating the traffic.

When nothing was forthcoming from the Pentagon after months of waiting, the author spent two half days at the National Archives in College Park, MD trying to learn if the traffic was there in the military records division.

On the second day, an Archives staffer indicated the traffic was indeed there on microfilm but at that point there was a plane to catch and a look at the microfilm was not possible.

On June 30, 2008, Sen. Inhofe sent a letter to the Archives asking assistance in locating the elusive communications.

Sen. Inhofe then received a letter dated July 28, 2008 from Timothy K. Nenninger, Chief, Archives II Reference

Section (NWCT2R), Textual Archives Services Division, which states:

"We searched the Subject Card Index (entry 10 NM-84) to the formerly Security Classified Correspondence, 1920–42, (Records of the War Department General and Special Staffs, Record Group 165) reproduced on microfilm Publication T1013 for references regarding awards, medals and the names Taylor and Welch, without success."

This was devastating news because it was the only piece of the puzzle missing among the various criteria (including citations and service records) required by the Army Medals Board for considering the upgrade of Ken Taylor and George Welch for the Medal of Honor.

Devastating news, but not surprising. It most likely can never be proved, but considering the two pilots were put forth as heroes in just six days the odds are Gen. Short in Hawaii and Gen. Marshall at the War Department did not wish to leave a paper trail on this action and the traffic was done by telephone.

And years ago the National Archives confirmed that Communiqué 19, the press release announcing the Taylor/Welch "first designated heroes status," is the only one missing among the sequence of similar documents of that time.

Although it's impossible to historically substantiate, even lesser medals such as the Bronze Star normally are not awarded by the military services in just a few days. Even the awarding of a Purple Heart for a combat injury takes some time for the appropriate paper work.

One notable exception is described in the late David Halberstam's "The Coldest Winter," when Gen.

MacArthur's hand-picked general in Korea, Ned Almond, choppered up near the Chosin Reservoir to keep pushing his commanders to drive north in spite of the overwhelming Chinese forces that had entered the war.

Halberstam writes:

"Then—for Almond loved nothing more than on-the-spot medal presentations—he announced that he had three Silver Stars he wanted to give out—one to (Lt. Col. Don Carlos) Faith and two to whomever Faith chose. Faith was appalled, but he thereupon chose a wounded lieutenant and asked him to come and stand at attention to get his medal. Just then the mess sergeant of Headquarters Company, George Stanley, walked by. Faith ordered him over. In front of a few men of Headquarters Company, the pathetic little medal ceremony took place. With that, Almond flew off in his helicopter. A moment later, Faith's operations officer, Maj. Wesley Curtis, walked over. 'What did the general say?' he asked.

"'You heard him, remnants fleeing north,' said an angry Faith as he ripped the medal off and threw it in the snow. One of his officers heard him say, 'What a damned travesty.'"

Here are some of the obvious flaws in the citations that came with the DSCs to Taylor and Welch:

Gen. Austin has said neither he nor to the best of his knowledge no one else in the 47th Squadron was either questioned or consulted about what Taylor and Welch did during the attack.

The citations appear to have been written by two different individuals with no one bothering to compare them or correct inconsistencies. For example, Taylor's citation mentions he was told to disperse his aircraft and not go up again. Welch's does not mention this order even though Taylor claimed his fellow pilot received the same instructions and the Welch testimony before the Roberts Commission confirms it.

The Welch citation describes his P-40 as having taken considerable fire from the Japanese planes. Taylor consistently stated that when the 47th planes landed back at Haleiwa after the action was over only his P-40 had been hit by enemy fire. Other squadron members have said they have no memory of any damage to the Welch P-40. The citation seems to be describing the combination of enemy fire taken by Taylor's P-40 and a P-36 flown by Lt. Philip Rasmussen of the 44th Pursuit Squadron.

While the citations for Taylor and Welch give each credit for shooting down several enemy aircraft, they do not say anything about what great damage these downed enemy planes likely saved at Pearl Harbor or other facilities. Numerous Medals of Honor have been awarded for saving of lives of other service people. There is no doubt but that by downing the enemy planes lives of military personnel were saved as well Navy vessels and military facilities were kept from being bombed and strafed.

Taylor's citation does not even mention he was wounded, usually a key factor in awarding a medal for heroism, and he was not presented a Purple Heart until months after the DSC award ceremony.

Welch's citation goes into considerable detail about his aerial combat that day. The awarding of medals usually requires witnesses to the heroism. Only Taylor was a witness to the Welch aerial combat. If he was not questioned, as he has told the author, then where did the person who wrote the citation get his information?

The Navy took months and even years before awarding the Congressional Medal of Honor to fifteen officers and enlisted men for heroism on Dec. 7. Ten of the fifteen MOH recipients died that day.

The Army and Marines awarded none.

The author has spent thousands of hours in the last decade researching the Taylor/Welch heroism in an effort to (1) restore their first hero status among historians and the media, and (2) trying to get both upgraded to the Congressional Medal of Honor.

The necessity for restoring their status as *first designated and decorated heroes* came about because of a factoid that emerged in 1941 and continues to this day.

According to one account sometime in the spring of 1942 the war was not going well, and President Roosevelt asked the War Department to produce a hero who would generate a great deal of publicity on the home front.

The Army came forward with the name of Capt. Colin Kelly Jr., a B-17 pilot who had gone down with his plane after the crew (except one member who was killed) had bailed out when the bomber was shot down trying to sink Japanese warships near the Philippines.

Capt. Kelly was posthumously awarded the Distinguished Service Cross and his story alone would have created some positive publicity.

But the White House in a stroke of genius also released a letter President Roosevelt wrote to whomever would be president in 1956, asking that Kelly's young son be given automatic admission to West Point when he reached that age.

In the media business it is a given that one cannot lose with a story about kids and animals. Thus with the addition of the presidential letter, the factoid that Capt. Kelly was the first hero was given new legs.

How this happened is quite amazing, because Capt. Kelly's heroic act did not occur until Dec. 10, 1941, which would indicate that there were no heroes during the Pearl Harbor attack three days earlier on Dec. 7.

Even as Taylor and Welch were being hailed across the country as "first heroes" of the new war in mid-December, 1941, the Army did not have to look far to find the factoid "first hero" in the person of Capt. Kelly.

In the Dec. 22, 1941 issue of Life Magazine it used two full pages of photos of 32 new "heroes." Most were killed on Dec. 7, 1941.

In the upper right-hand corner of the second page is a large photo of Capt. Colin Kelly Jr.

The text reads, "The bravery of Captain Colin Kelly Jr. (right) on *December* 12 *(sic) off Luzon in the Philippines provided America with its first war hero.*"

The text and the caption under Capt. Kelly's photo both state that his B-17 sank the Japanese battleship Haruma. Later it was found the Haruma at the time was a thousand miles away.

And as an example of the scope of this factoid, the official U.S. Air Force Museum web site at Wright-Patterson AFB until recently had a page with a painting of Capt.

Kelly along with copy designating him as the first hero of World War II. The copy was changed after the error was brought to the attention of officials there by the author.

Getting Taylor and Welch upgraded from the DSCs to the Medal of Honor is another matter.

The very small crack in the door of reasons for an upgrade by the Army Medals Board is if an error was committed by the Army high command when it recommended the two pilots for the DSC instead of the MOH.

The error would be that the awarding of medals to Taylor and Welch was done in such haste to divert attention from the Army's disaster in Hawaii there was not time to thoroughly evaluate the extent of their heroism. That would include having quickly taken off on their own for the first flight, to have shot down bombers probably headed for targets at Pearl Harbor and for having gone up a second time knowing they were vastly outnumbered by the Japanese and against orders from superiors.

In considering Taylor's and Welch's extraordinary heroism, their citations should be evaluated within the perspective of the fifteen MOH citations for the Navy heroes.

The reason for this evaluation is that in the twenty-three years of peacetime between World War I and World War II a minimum of medals was awarded, and the criteria should be as much alike as possible and not based on the many other MOHs later awarded during that war.

To put this evaluation in perspective, Gen. Austin said that when he heard his two pilots were being awarded the DSCs he really did not know that much about medals for heroism.

Gen. Taylor also said that back then he did not have a full appreciation of what the DSC meant.

Both Taylor and Welch thought they had downed more Japanese planes than the number for which they received credit. But it is almost certain the Army made no effort to find witnesses who might have confirmed these kills.

Taking time for a thorough investigation, especially among personnel at the Ewa Marine base, might have found witnesses to Taylor's belief that two planes he downed fell into the ocean. At least this was the Navy's approach in its awarding of the Medal of Honor to fifteen recipients which in some cases took years.

On Aug. 9, 2008, the author received an email from David Aiken, director, Pearl Harbor History Associates, Inc. stating that "My study has finally confirmed the four planes, by crew and crash which Ken Taylor shot down." Combined with his one kill at Guadalcanal, this would have given Taylor the coveted status of an ace which he never was given before his death. (The scrapbook Taylor's mother kept has a certificate awarded her son for shooting down a plane over Guadalcanal.)

The same effort also might have added to Welch's kills, which would have given him the status of being the first ace of World War II. He said in his testimony before the Roberts Commission he had been credited with shooting down five enemy planes.

The key element for the award of an MOH involves witnesses to extraordinary heroism.

The author's contact with 47th Squadron survivors produced not a single person who knew more than that Taylor and Welch went up twice and did shoot down some of the enemy planes.

But there is one major exception supporting George Welch's upgrade.

In the hour-long video interview the author did with Gen. Taylor on Nov. 19, 2001, he describes what he and Welch did that day including his buddy picking off the Japanese plane on his tail early in the second flight.

Therefore, there is at least one witness to the Welch heroism through Gen. Taylor's story.

These are some of the other developments post-Pearl Harbor.

Ken Taylor went on to have a career in the Air Force, retiring at the rank of colonel from the Pentagon in 1967. He then returned to Anchorage, Alaska where he had served in the Alaska Air Command.

He first became adjutant for the Alaska Air National Guard and was in the insurance business. His second military retirement came as a brigadier general and commander of the Alaska Air Guard.

At some point the Taylors bought a home in a retirement community in the Tucson area where they spent the winters.

Near the time of the 60th anniversary of Pearl Harbor after leaving Anchorage to spend the winter in Arizona, Gen. Taylor received an envelope in the mail.

When he opened it, out fell a dozen or so thin, tooth-pick-like brass shards.

The note inside was from former Sgt. Raymond Turley of Mt. Sterling, Kentucky, who had served as a crew chief for the 47th Squadron.

"These are pieces of the bullet I found when I cleaned up your plane at Wheeler Field on Monday after the Pearl Harbor attack," Turley wrote. "I thought that after sixty years you should have them."

Taylor described the bullet as having hit the trim tab in his P-40 cockpit, which is a round piece of metal about the size of half a grapefruit, perhaps two and a half inches thick, and level with the pilot's left elbow.

Thus the round came from a Japanese plane, probably a Zero, diving from above and behind him, glanced off the trim tab and went through Taylor's left arm on a trajectory that sent it to the lower part of the cockpit where it exploded with some of the pieces causing minor wounds to his legs.

"It certainly did not do my tux pants any good," Taylor remembered. "But the only real damage was to my ego because I mistakenly thought we were better than those guys."

The week of Dec. 7, the 47th along with the few serviceable aircraft that survived the attack at the other Army Air Corps bases of Hickam and Bellows fields, were on high alert and flying missions searching for any signs of Japanese aircraft or vessels.

At the Officers5 Club in the evenings Taylor and Welch kept to themselves and other 47th squadron pilots interviewed said they never discussed what happened in the air on Dec. 7.

Ken Taylor did develop a fondness for Miss Flora Love Morrison, the blonde he had met before the Pearl Harbor attack. They were married May 9, 1942, in Honolulu.

Taylor was sent to Guadalcanal and shot down one enemy plane before breaking a leg when someone jumped on top of him in a foxhole during an air raid.

He died Nov. 25, 2006 at the age of 86 at an assisted living facility in Tucson, Arizona, and was interred in Arlington National Cemetery.

George Welch also was in time sent to the South Pacific where he claimed 12 more enemy planes downed for a total of 16, making him one of the top 35 aces in the Pacific Theater during World War II.

In addition to his Distinguished Service Cross, Welch was awarded the Distinguished Flying Cross, the Silver Star and Air Medal, making him one of the most decorated heroes of World War II.

He left the Air Force in 1944 because of malaria and was married to a young woman from Australia.

Ten years later as chief test pilot for North American Aviation, Welch was killed while flying an F-100 at Edwards Air Force Base.

On Sept. 15, 2007, he was posthumously inducted into the Aerospace Walk of Honor at Lancaster, California, near Edwards along with four other former test pilots including Navy Capt. Bob Crippen, former NASA Shuttle commander.

While it may not be necessary, it seems appropriate to end this book with some information and observations about what might have been done to prevent the vast extent of death and destruction from the attack on Pearl Harbor.

Only a few days after the Dec. 7. attack both Adm. Kimmel, the top Navy commander, and Gen. Short, head of the Army in Hawaii, were relieved of their commands and not long after both retired.

Both were reduced one grade in rank upon retirement.

All the investigations from the Roberts Commission in 1941–42 on through the Pentagon's Dorn Commission in 1995 concluded Kimmel and Short had not provided the leadership expected of them in their high positions at the time of the attack. The Dorn report did bring into question decisions and actions not taken by President Roosevelt and Gen. Marshall that might have motivated Kimmel and Short to have had their commands on high alert. But no evidence has ever been found that Roosevelt concealed knowledge of the impending attack just for a reason to enter into a war with Japan.

After Adm. Kimmel and Gen. Short were relieved of their commands when the Roberts Commission concluded there had been "dereliction of duty" by the two commanders in not having their personnel better prepared for an attack on Hawaii, each had a different reaction to this black mark on their long careers.

Gen. Short accepted the decision but Adm. Kimmel mounted an effort to clear his name. That effort is still carried on by his descendents, which resulted in the latest study in 1995 called the "Dorn Report" but no change in his status.

One problem with both commanders is that they, through their own public relations activities in the months and days just before Dec. 7, 1941, set themselves up for an unfortunate fall and actually provided the "smoking gun" making their alibis that they had been left out of the intelligence loop irrelevant.

Earlier in this book Gen. Short is quoted from a radio address on May 20, 1941 as having said, *"I think we can meet with confidence all threats of enemy encroachment even that of bombardment from the air."*

Yet on the "date that will live in infamy" his Army Air Corps was not on alert with many of its personnel scattered all over the island.

Adm. Kimmel also had set himself up in a situation that at the time looked like a major public relations coup, but after Dec. 7 placed him in a position of ridicule.

A few weeks before the Pearl Harbor attack he had been persuaded to pose for a photo, in his white uniform with all its gold braid, standing under the sixteen-inch guns of a battleship with binoculars in hand staring at some distant object.

This color photograph became the cover of the popular Look Magazine for its November 18, 1941 issue.

One of the headlines on the cover read, "U.S. Navy Has a New Plan to Fight Japan."

The headline was a reference to an article inside by Hallett Abend, a Pulitzer Prize winning New York Times correspondent on Far Eastern affairs, entitled, "How the U.S. Navy will fight Japan."

While Abend showed his ample expertise in various observations about naval warfare and the rise of air power in battles by both the Germans and Japanese, there was one damning paragraph predicting the defense of Hawaii by Adm. Kimmel's Pacific fleet.

"When the clash comes," Abend wrote, "the Japanese fleet will have to stay in home waters, to guard the islands of the Empire against naval raids. Our own fleet will cruise somewhere west of Hawaii, with scout planes far over the seas day and night to prevent surprise raids on the Pearl Harbor naval base or our own West Coast cities."

Thus by appearing on the cover of Look and associating himself with Mr. Abend's article and predictions, Adm. Kimmel apparently provided the journalist with his strategy for the Navy fleet in the Pacific. There is no evidence the author could find where Adm. Kimmel tried to correct this assessment of his strategy.

While there was no clash until the Japanese surprise attack, there also was no fleet cruising somewhere "west of Hawaii with scout planes far over the seas day and night" as Mr. Abend wrote in the article.

One of Yamamoto's cleverest decisions was to approach Oahu from the north while those aircraft and surface warships searching for the Japanese task force after the attack looked to the south.

Information on Yamamoto's task force was not found by the Pearl Harbor code breakers because it was carried on with such secrecy there was no code to break.

True, Adm. Halsey's carrier task force was at sea but it was returning from delivering planes to Wake Island and not cruising around to protect Pearl Harbor and other Hawaiian military facilities. Instead most of the fleet was anchored in Pearl Harbor not on high alert but just sitting ducks for the Japanese bombers and fighters.

And had Halsey's task force been unlucky enough to run into the Yamamoto armada, all his ships would have been sunk with the loss of hundreds of lives.

Earlier it has been written here that absent the latest information about negotiations with Japan, common sense on the part of Kimmel and Short would have seemed to transcend lack of intelligence reports early in December.

Not to minimize the various official investigations of the U.S. military's lack of preparations for a possible aerial attack by Japan, there seems to have been abundant warnings from one simple and easily accessible source–the Honolulu newspapers.

We have to assume Adm. Kimmel, Gen. Short and their top advisors did read the Honolulu Advertiser and/ or Bulletin on a daily basis. Or maybe not.

If one were to go to the Hawaii State Library in Honolulu and read the newspapers on microfilm for the week preceding the attack, dozens of stories would seem to have given ample warning to Kimmel and Short to place all forces in Hawaii on high alert. Examples of the headlines have been used at the end of the various days or chapters.

But here are just a few from the Honolulu Advertiser:

"Hull (U.S. Secretary of State), Japanese Envoys in Crucial Confab Today." Dec. 1, 1941.

'JAPAN GIVES TWO WEEKS MORE, Prepares For Action In Event Of Failure." Dec. 2, 1941.

"Philippines Declared In Great Peril." Dec. 3, 1941.

"Japanese Pin Blame on U.S." (if a war starts in the Pacific) Dec. 4, 1941.

"COMPLETE COLLAPSE OF US-JAPAN TALKS LOOM." Dec. 5, 1941.

That said, the unfortunate fate of Adm. Kimmel and Gen. Short in a way is reminiscent of the ending of Herman Wouk's wonderful stage play, "The Caine Mutiny Court Martial."

The Caine, an old Navy minesweeper, was crewed with one exception by a group of young officers who gradually convinced themselves that the ship's old man, Capt. Queeg, was crazy and to save the ship in a typhoon they needed to mutiny and take command of the vessel.

Back in San Francisco, Lt. Steve Maryk, the officer who actually relieved Capt. Queeg (dubbed 'Old Yellowstain' by Lt. Keefer, one of the officers) as captain of the ship, was charged with mutiny and went through a court martial. Defending Maryk was a Jewish Navy pilot and lawyer who had seen some action himself.

Arriving at the party in the Fairmont Hotel where the officers are celebrating Maryk's acquittal and Keefer's having sold a novel about the war, Lt. Barney Greenwald, the lawyer for Maryk, is in no mood for celebration.

The officers all start yelling for Greenwald, who is drunk, to make a speech.

"So when all hell broke loose and the Germans started running out of soap and figured, well, time to come over and melt down Mrs. Greenwald (his mother)," Lt. Greenwald tells them, "who's gonna stop 'em? Not her boy Barney. Can't stop a Nazi with a law book. So I dropped the lawbooks, and ran to learn how to fly. Stout fellow. "Meantime, and it took a year and a half before I was any good, who was keeping Mama out of the soap dish? Tom Keefer? Communications school. Willie Keith? Midshipman school. Old Yellowstain, maybe? Why, yes, even poor sad Queeg. And most of them not sad at all, fellows, a lot of them sharper boys than any of us, don't kid yourself, you can't be good in the Army or Navy unless you're goddam good. Though maybe not up on Proust, 'n' *Finnegan's Wake*, 'n' all."

It had been Keefer the intellectual who had over several months goaded Maryk into the mutiny, feeding him bits of pop psychology that helped raise doubts about Capt. Queeg's sanity.

When Lt. Greenwald finishes his speech, he throws his glass of wine in Keefer's face and leaves.

As with Capt. Queeg, Adm. Kimmel and Gen. Short had long and honorable careers in their services. They had eschewed other paths where they might have ended up as corporate CEOs or in other civilian jobs where they probably would have been paid more money than each earned through the years as officers in the military. As Lt. Greenwald said, "you can't be good in the Army or Navy unless you're goddam good."

Instead they chose careers in the military to defend our country in times of peril.

So they made mistakes of judgment in not having had their forces better prepared for a possible attack by the Japanese. But at least they were there and both paid dearly for having been "regulars," while millions of their contemporaries were, as with the officers in the cast of "The Caine Mutiny Court Martial," studying law, in communication school, on the playing fields of Princeton or in Midshipman school.

For Adm. Kimmel, Gen. Short and all others who chose the path of serving with the military in the peacetime services and were in harm's way when World War II started on Dec. 7, 1941, our nation should forever be grateful. Pearl Harbor was a tragic event. But even those who suffered and suffered losses that day should be able to see it certainly would have been far, far worse but for such heroes as Ken Taylor and George Welch.

Appendices

DSC Citation for Second Lt. George S. Welch, first designated and decorated hero of World War II

GEORGE S. WELCH, Second Lieutenant, 47th Pursuit Squadron, 15th Pursuit Group, Air Corps, United States Army.

For extraordinary heroism in action over the Island of Oahu, Territory of Hawaii, and waters adjacent thereto, December 7, 1941. When surprised by a heavy air attack by Japanese Forces on Wheeler Field and vicinity at approximately 8 a.m., he left Wheeler Field and proceeded by automobile, under fire, to Haleiwa Landing Field, a distance of approximately ten miles, where the planes of his Squadron were stationed. He immediately, on his own initiative, took off for the purpose of attacking the invading Japanese aircraft in attacking force, and proceeded to his initial point over Barbers Point. At time of take off he was armed only with caliber .30 machine guns. Upon arrival over Barbers Point he observed a formation of approximately twelve planes over Ewa, about one thousand feet below and ten miles away. Accompanied only by one other pursuit ship, he immediately attacked this enemy formation and shot down an enemy dive bomber with one burst from three caliber .30 guns. At this point he discovered that one caliber.30 gun was jammed. While engaged in combat his plane was hit by an incendiary bullet, which passed through the baggage compartment just in the rear of his seat. He climbed above the clouds, checked his plane, returned to the attack over Barbers Point, and immediately attacked a Japanese plane running out to sea, which he shot down, the plane falling into the ocean. No more enemy planes being in sight he proceeded to Wheeler Field to refuel and replenish ammunition. Just as refueling and reloading were completed but before his guns had been repaired, a second wave of about fifteen enemy planes approached low over Wheeler Field. Three came at him and he immediately took off, headed straight into the attack, and went to the assistance of a brother officer, who was being attacked from the rear. This enemy plane burst into flames and crashed about half way between Wahiawa and Haleiwa. During this combat his plane was struck by three bullets from the rear gun of the ship he was attacking. One strikng his motor, one the propeller and one the cowling. This attack wave having disappeared, he returned to the vicinity of Ewa and found one enemy plane proceeding seaward, which he pursued and shot down about five miles off shore, immediately thereafter returning to his station at Haleiwa Landing Field. Lieutenant WELCH'S initiative, presence of mind, coolness under fire against overwhelming odds in his first battle, expert maneuvering of his plane, and determined action contributed to a large extent toward driving off this sudden unexpected enemy air attack. Address: Care of the Adjutant General,

Washington, D.C. Entered Military Service from Delaware.

By order of the Secretary of War

G.G. Marshal, Chief of Staff

DSC Citation for 2nd Lt. Kenneth M. Taylor, second designated and decorated hero of World War II.

Kenneth M. Taylor, second Lieutenant, 47th Pursuit Squadron, 15th Pursuit Group, Air Corps, United States Army. For extraordinary heroism in action over the Island of Oahu, Territory of Hawaii, and waters adjacent thereto, December 7, 1941. When surprised by a heavy air attack by Japanese forces on Wheeler Field and vicinity at approximately 8 a.m., he left Wheeler Field and proceeded by automobile, under fire, to Haleiwa Landing Field, a distance of approximately ten miles, where the planes of his squadron were stationed. He immediately, on his own initiative, took off for the purpose of attacking the invading forces, without first obtaining information as to the number of planes in the attacking force, and proceeded to his initial point over Barbers Point. At time of take-off his plane was equipped with caliber .30 machine guns only. Upon arrival over Barbers Point, he observed a formation of approximately twelve planes over Ewa, about one thousand feet below and ten miles away.

Accompanied by only one other pursuit ship he immediately attacked this enemy formation and shot down two enemy planes. No more enemy planes being in sight he proceeded to Wheeler Field to refuel and replenish ammunition. Just as reloading was completed but before ammunition boxes had been removed a second wave of enemy planes attacked Wheeler Field, approaching directly toward him at low altitude. Although Lieutenant Taylor had been advised that he should not go up again he made a quick take-off ending in a chandelle, thereby saving his plane as he escaped from a superior force of eight to ten planes by climbing into the clouds. Lieutenant Taylor's initiative, presence of mind, coolness under fire against overwhelming odds in his first battle, expert maneuvering of his plane, and determined action contributed to a large extent toward driving off this sudden, unexpected enemy air attack.

By order of the Secretary of War
G.G. Marshall, Chief of Staff

Author's Note: While doing research in the military records division of the National Archives in College Park, MD, on May 20, 2008, I was going through Gen. George C. Marshall's personal correspondence file during the days following the Pearl Harbor attack. Most of the letters, carbon copies on onionskin paper, were mundane correspondence with people offering their dogs for the war effort and that kind of thing. But one document stood out because it was on a legal-size sheet of paper and for its content. I thought it might be interesting reading if included here. In truth, according to "At Dawn We Slept" by Gordon W. Prange, Donald M. Goldstein and Katherine V. Dillon, Ichiro Fuji was none other than Herr Doktor Bernard Julius Otto Kuehn, a German who had lived in Honolulu several years prior to the Dec. 7, 1941 attack under contract as a spy for the Japanese intelligence operation.

SECRET, First Priority, DECEMBER 12, 1941
COMMANDING GENERAL
HAWAIIAN DEPARTMENT
HONOLULU, TER OF HAWAII
FOR YOUR INFORMATION AND NECESSARY ACTION COLON ONE ICHIRO FUJI ON DECEMBER THIRD ARRANGED FOLLOWING SIGNAL SYSTEM FOR JAPANESE FLEET UPON CLOSURE NORMAL MEANS COMMUNICATION. LANIKAI BEACH HOUSE TO SHOW LIGHTS BETWEEN EIGHT PM AND MIDNIGHT AND BETWEEN MIDNIGHT AND FOUR AM WITH VARIOUS MEANINGS AS TO OUR NAVAL

DISPOSITIONS DEPENDING ON THE HOUR OF DISPLAY PERIOD SIMILARLY A STAR AND A ROMAN NUMERAL THREE AT THE HEAD OF THE SAIL OF THE QUOTE STAR BOAT UNQUOTE IN LANIKAI BAY DURING DAYLIGHT STOP ALSO LIGHTS IN THE ATTICK WINDOW OF KALAMA HOUSE PARENTHESIS BEACH VILLAGE ONE MILE NORTH WEST OF LANIKAI CLOSE PARENTHESIS STOP ALSO ADVERTISEMENTS BROADCAST ON KGMG RE CHINESE RUG FOR Sale COMMA CHIC ... CO FARM COMMA BEAUTY OPERATOR ALL APPLY P O BOX 1476 STOP IF ABOVE/UNWORKABLE A SIGNAL BONFIRE TO BE LOCATED ON MARIE SIX MILES NORTH OF KULA SANITORIUM AT POINT HALFWAY BETWEEN LOWER KULA ROAD AND HALEAKALA ROAD.

MARSHALL

This was delivered personally to message center (Colonel French in pencil draft Col. Bratton) G-2 at 10:10 a.m. December 12.

SECRET

Bibliographical Summary

Had I known I would be writing a book some day about Ken Taylor and George Welch and their heroics at Pearl Harbor when I began my research in 2001, I would have planned to provide a bibliography in the traditional manner.

But the idea of a book on Taylor and Welch did not arrive until it was suggested by Daniel Martinez, Pearl Harbor historian, at a dinner in May, 2007 in Honolulu. By then it was too late to be academic.

In the meantime file drawers began to fill up, dozens of calls made, emails and letters written, trips made to Hawaii and the National Archives in College Park, Maryland, books and videos read and watched along with information that came from various sources.

Reviewing the major sources over the years, this is a listing that substantiates not only material in this book but that used when I began building the www.pearlharborhero.net web site in June, 2006. To date, after thousands of hits by those interested in the Pearl Harbor story no one has yet questioned any statement in it.

Aiken, Daniel, Pearl Harbor History Associates. Confirmation by email dated Aug. 9, 2008 of his evidence of two additional planes downed by Lt. Taylor on Dec. 7, 1941, giving him a total of four kills.

Air Force Historical Agency, Maxwell AFB, Alabama

I first contacted the Air Force Historical Agency at Maxwell Air Force Base to see how many planes Taylor had downed since he had said it was two certain and he thought two others had fallen into the ocean near Barber's Point. The eventual response from Maxwell was he was credited with two. This caused further confusion because the inscription on the plaque by the mockup P-40 that Twentieth Century Fox donated to Wheeler Field after filming parts of the movie "Tora! Tora! Tora!" there credited Ken with four downed. But apparently AFHA has the final say on this matter.

Books

Arakaki, Leatrice R. and Kuborn, John R., *7 DECEMBER 1941 THE AIR FORCE STORY*, Government Printing Office, 1991.

Arroyo, Ernest, *Pearl Harbor*, MetroBooks, 2001.

Borch, Fred and Martinez, Daniel, *Kimmel, Short and Pearl Harbor*, Naval Institute Press, 2005.

Gailey, Harry A., *The War in the Pacific From Pearl Harbor to Tokyo Bay*, Presidio Press, 1995.

Halberstam, David, *The Coldest Winter*, Hyperion, 2007.

Lord, Walter, *DAY OF INFAMY*, Holt, 1957. It should be noted that while Mr. Lord in researching material for this outstanding work interviewed many Pearl Harbor survivors for first-hand accounts of the attack, Lts. Taylor and Welch are not on the list of interviewees.

Prange, Gordon W., In Collaboration With Donald M. Goldstein and Katherine V. Dillon, *At Dawn We Slept The Untold Story of Pearl Harbor*, MCGRAW-HILL BOOK COMPANY, 1981.

Prange, Gordon W. with Donald M. Goldstein and Katherine V. Dillon, *Dec. 7 1941 THE DAY THE JAPANESE ATTACKED PEARL HARBOR*, Warner Books, 1988.

Prange, Gordon W. with Donald M. Goldstein and Katherine V. Dillon, *God's Samurai–LEAD PILOT AT PEARL HARBOR*, Brasseys's Inc., 1990.

Scott, Robert L. Jr., *Damned To Glory*, Blue Ribbon Books, 1944.

Weintraub, Stanley, *LONG DAY'S JOURNEY INTO WAR DECEMBER 7, 1941*, TRUMAN TALLEY BOOKS/ PLUME, 1991.

Smithsonian, *December 7, 1941*, Harper-Collins Publishers 2006.

Weintraub, Stanley, *LONG DAY'S JOURNEY INTO WAR*, Penguin Books USA, Inc., 1991.

Wels, Susan, *December 7, 1941 Pearl Harbor America's Darkest Day*, Tehabi Books, Inc., 2001.

Willmot, H.P. with Tohmatsu and W Spencer Johnson, *PEARL HARBOR*, Cassell & Co., 2001.

Congressional Medal of Honor Society.

Consultation with various staff members over several years.

Documentaries, Television Programs and Videos.

Live from Pearl Harbor 60th Anniversary Special, The History Channel, Dec. 7, 2001.

NBC Evening News, December 7, 2003, story on Gen. Taylor's heroism.

National Geographic's *Ultimate World War II Collection* with a disc on the Pearl Harbor attack narrated by Tom Brokaw, former NBC anchor.

Pearl Harbor, The History Channel, A&E Television Networks, 2000.

PEARL HARBOR Surprise Attack!, Best Film and Video Corp. 1987.

PEARL HARBOR THE EYEWITNESS STORY, CRT Partners, 1995.

C-Span, Symposium on Adm. Kimmel, Dec. 7, 1999, sponsored by the Navy Historical Foundation at the Navy Memorial, Washington, DC.

Wheeler Field black and white video of the decoration ceremony for Taylor and Welch provided to Gen. Taylor by the late Historian Stephen Ambrose.

20th Century Fox Movietone News newsreel of the Wheeler Field decoration ceremony for Taylor and Welch.

Pearl Harbor, The History Channel, A&E Television Networks, 2000.

Films

Tora! Tora! Tora!, Twentieth Century-Fox, 1970.

Pearl Harbor, Touchstone Pictures, 2001.

Air Force Personnel

Farfour, Col. George USAF, *Research on Gen. Ken Taylor's Heroism On December 7, 1941 When Pearl Harbor Was Attacked.* At the time then Maj. Farfour began his research project on Gen. Taylor he called to ask his cooperation.

Gen. Taylor suggested it would be best for Maj. Farfour to work with this author and that was an acceptable arrangement with both of us. My major contribution to the Farfour research was providing him a copy of the Taylor scrapbook. When Maj. Farfour completed his project, he then provided me a copy of his work which contained the Taylor/Welch testimony before the Roberts Commission and other information that was immensely helpful in my research.

Individual Interviews

Austin, Maj. Gen. Gordon USAF Ret., commander of the 47th Pursuit Squadron on Dec. 7, 1941. My first interview with Gen. Austin was on video at the Arizona Inn in Tucson in the spring of 2002. Since that time I conducted a long interview with the general in his home in the Washington, DC area in November, 2007 at which time he graciously loaned me his personal files from the 1941 era, and we also have talked many times on the phone regarding issues surrounding the attack.

Dougherty, Gen. Russell USAF Ret.

Elia, Adam, historian, 25th Division, U.S. Army, Wheeler Field.

Henze, Lt. Col. Irvin USAF Ret., pilot with the 47th Pursuit Squadron on Dec. 7, 1941.

Jones, Syd, Pacific Air Museum, Ford Island, Pearl Harbor. .

Klapakis, Donna, civilian public affairs officer, Wheeler Field.

Martinez, Daniel, Pearl Harbor Historian.

Norberg, John, Purdue University staff and author of "Wings of Their Dreams," a book about the numerous astronauts who have studied at Purdue and includes information on George Welch who left there to join the Army Air Corps.

Sweeney, Stuart "Bud," a private with the 19th Group and ground crewman who tried to rearm Lt. Taylor's P-40 with .50 caliber ammunition at Wheeler Field after his first flight on Dec. 7, 1941.

Taylor, B. Gen. Kenneth M. USAF Ret., pilot with the 47th Pursuit Squadron on Dec. 7, 1941.

Taylor, Mrs. Kenneth M., who had met Lt. Taylor prior to Dec. 7, 1941, and was in Hawaii during the Japanese attack.

Turley, Raymond, former sergeant and crew chief with the 47th Pursuit Squadron, U.S. Army Air Corps, in Hawaii on Dec. 7, 1941.

Tyler, Lt. Col. Kermit USAF Ret., operations officer on duty during the Japanese attack on Dec. 7, 1941.

Welch, Giles, son of 2nd Lt. George Welch, pilot in the 47th Pursuit Squadron on Dec. 7, 1941.

Welch, Peter, nephew of George Welch.

Coles, Williaam, Honolulu Advertiser reporter.

Libraries

Franklin D. Roosevelt Presidential Library and Museum, Hyde Park, New York.

Hawaii State Library, Honolulu

Tulsa Oklahoma Public Library

University of Arizona Library

Pima County, AZ Library

Periodicals

Life Magazine, December 22, 1941. Life (not military officials) declares Capt. Colin Kelly Jr. as America's first war hero when he was killed December 12, 1941 in action off Luzon in the Philippines.

Life Magazine, Feb. 16, 1942 with drawings of Taylor and Welch and a story on their heroism.

Life Magazine, July 13, 1942, with photograph of Lt. George Welch with heroes from other Allied countries surrounded by female Hollywood stars at the end of a cross-country tour boosting morale for the war.

Look Magazine, November 18, 1941. Adm. Kimmel, Commander of the U.S. Fleet on the cover and *How the U.S. Navy will fight Japan*, an article by Hallett Abend.

National Geographic, December 1991, *PEARL HARBOR A RETURN TO THE DAY OF INFAMY* by Thomas B. Allen and Photographs by David Doubilet.

People Magazine, May 28, 2001, *Moment of Truth*, article about survivors of the Pearl Harbor attack including information and photographs of Gen. Ken. Taylor and George Welch.

The Sooner Magazine, January 1942, with Second Lieutenant Kenneth M. Taylor on the cover and information on him in an article, *Sooners at Home and Abroad*.

National Archives

Dorr, Robert F., Article entitled *Fighting Back, The Army Air Forces at Pearl Harbor*.

Letter confirming the War Department's Communiqué No. 19 issued on Dec. 13, 1941 is the only communiqué of that time frame missing from the records.

Letter confirming traffic between Lt. Gen. Short of the Army high command in Hawaii and the U.S. War Dept.

in Washington, DC. concerning awarding of medals to Lts. Ken Taylor and George Welch does not exist there.

Video of Wheeler Field pilots who shot down at least one Japanese plane during the Dec. 7, 1941 attack being congratulated by a senior officer.

Photographs of Lts. Ken Taylor and George Welch.

Newspaper Archival Services.

The New York Times and the Daily Oklahoman.

Play Script

Wouk, Herman, *The Caine Mutiny Court-Martial*, A DRAMA IN TWO ACTS, Samuel French, Inc. 1954, 1955, 1982, 1983.

Taylor Family Scrapbook. This is no ordinary scrapbook, kept by Mrs. Joe Taylor as a record of Ken Taylor, her son, and his early career in the Army Air Corps and later the U.S. Air Force. It is about four inches thick with pages now very delicate with mostly newspaper and magazine articles. The covers are made of varnished plywood with a professionally painted logo of Brooks Field, where Ken Taylor received his pilot's silver wings and second lieutenant's gold bars.

Pasted on one of the first pages of the scrapbook is the United Press story from Washington, DC with a typo in the date of Dec. 19, 1941. The story is about the War Department issuing a press release called "Communiqué No. 19" in which

Lts. Ken Taylor and George Welch were designated as the first heroes of World War II and would be awarded the Distinguished Service Cross for their heroic action during the Japanese attack on Hawaii on Dec. 7, 1941.

This UP story really was moved across the country on Dec. 13, 1941. The scrapbook has adequate proof that this was the correct date. This proof includes a telegram from the UP bureau in Oklahoma City dated Dec. 13 asking a newspaper that covered the area of the Joe Taylor home in Hominy, Oklahoma to provide additional information on the newly named hero. The book also includes stories from the Daily Oklahoman and other newspapers dated Dec. 14, 1941 carrying the Taylor heroism story.

U.S. Army

Letter to U.S. Sen. James Inhofe from the Army Medals Board listing the criteria for an upgrade to the Congressional Medal of Honor for Gen. Ken Taylor.

U.S. Army Museum of Hawaii

Various communications in person and via emails with Ms. Judy Bowman, Curator.

JOHN MARTIN MEEK has worn the uniforms of the Army, Navy and Marines. He earned his BA from the University of Oklahoma and MA from Syracuse University. He taught at The American University and the University of Virginia. He is the author of *The Christmas Hour* and *I Might Just Be Right*.

www.pearlharborhero.net